"The Potter-Efrons continue to capture the essence of anger through their anger styles. By understanding the eleven anger styles and how they relate to each of us in a personal way, we gain insight that can unlock our own chains of anger. The Potter-Efrons have generously provided the tools to help break away from the most hardened of anger styles. Their guidance and experience will give each of us the opportunity to begin our journey on a path towards emotional freedom."

—V. William Blount, MS, author of *Healthy Anger*

"This book offers detailed, yet accessible, descriptions of anger styles, followed by easy-to-understand alternatives to healthier expressions. Anyone who wants to examine their anger will be able to find themselves in this book."

—Susan C. Turell, Ph.D., counseling psychologist
working with survivors of sexual and physical violence

LETTING
GO OF
ANGER

SECOND EDITION

The Eleven Most
Common Anger Styles &
What to Do About Them

Ronald T. Potter-Efron, MSW, Ph.D.
Patricia S. Potter-Efron, MS

New Harbinger Publications, Inc.

Distributed in Canada by Raincoast Books

Copyright © 2006 by Ron Potter-Efron and Pat Potter-Efron
New Harbinger Publications, Inc.
5674 Shattuck Avenue
Oakland, CA 94609

Cover design by Amy Shoup; Acquired by Catharine Sutker; Edited by Kayla Sussell; Text design by Tracy Marie Carlson

Library of Congress Cataloging-in-Publication Data

Potter-Efron, Ronald T.
Letting go of anger : the eleven most common anger styles and what to do about them / Ronald T. Potter-Efron and Patricia S. Potter-Efron. — 2nd ed.
p. cm.
ISBN-13: 978-1-57224-448-1
ISBN-10: 1-57224-448-8
1. Anger. 2. Control (Psychology) I. Potter-Efron, Patricia S. II. Title.
BF575.A5P85 2006
152.4'7—dc22
2006014692

09   08   07
10   9   8   7   6   5   4

For David Allan Keith
newest member of our family when first written,
now in double digits

Contents

I

Introduction

1

Anger Problems, Anger Styles

Once upon a time a young couple climbed a high mountain. There they saw a wise old man. He motioned for them to sit. He told them they could ask him any questions.

They asked him the meaning of life. He told them.

They asked him the recipe for happiness. He wrote it down.

They asked him about all the secrets of the universe. No problem.

Then they asked him a *hard* question: "Oh, Great Master, we are angry so often. We hurt each other when we get angry. What can we do?"

Suddenly the master glared at them, broke his pencil in two, cursed loudly, and stomped back into his cave. "Alas," he muttered over his shoulder, "if I could figure that out I wouldn't be sitting here all alone on this mountain!"

WHAT DO YOU DO WHEN YOU GET ANGRY?

Nobody really knows what to do with their anger, at least not all the time. Anger is a gift, a natural part of the human condition, but it isn't easy to handle. Anger causes a lot of trouble in our lives.

This book is about how people deal with their anger. We'll talk later in this chapter about "healthy" anger—what it looks and feels like, how to use it, how to let it go. Your relationship with anger is "healthy" when you deal with it in this way—you recognize it, you act on it, and you let it go.

Most of this book, though, is about anger problems and anger styles. An *anger problem* is something that makes it hard for you to handle your anger. Examples are being afraid of your anger, liking it too much, "stuffing" your anger because you don't know how to express it out loud, and exploding in rage.

An *anger style* is a pattern, a particular way you handle your anger. The style you choose answers this question: "What do I do when I get angry?"

We describe eleven anger styles in this book. There are more, but these eleven are common. You may find yourself in one of them or several. As we write, we'll mention the good parts of each style, its problems, and what you can do to change if you are stuck in that style.

Before we go on, though, we'd like you to take the brief quiz that follows. There are thirty-three Yes/No questions. Just answer them quickly, without worrying too much about doing it right.

Anger Styles Quiz

1. I try never to get angry.   Yes   No

2. I get really nervous when others are angry.   Yes   No

3. I feel I'm doing something bad when I get angry.   Yes   No

- .

4. I often tell people I'll do what they want, but   Yes   No
    then I forget.

5. I frequently say things like "Yeah, but ..." and   Yes   No
    "I'll do it later."

6. People tell me I must be angry but I'm not   Yes   No
    sure why.

- .

7. I get mad at myself a lot.   Yes   No

8. I "stuff" my anger and then get headaches, a stiff   Yes   No
    neck, stomachaches, etc.

9. I freqently call myself ugly names like "dummy,   Yes   No
    selfish," etc.

- .

10. My anger comes on really fast.   Yes   No

11. I act before I think when I get angry.   Yes   No

12. My anger goes away very quickly.   Yes   No

- .

13. I get very angry when people criticize me.   Yes   No

14. People say I am easily hurt and oversensitive.   Yes   No

15. I get angry easily when I feel bad about myself.   Yes   No

- .

16. I get mad in order to get what I want.   Yes   No

17. I try to scare others with my anger.   Yes   No

18. I sometimes pretend to be mad when I'm not   Yes   No
     really angry.

- -

19. Sometimes I get angry just for the excitement   Yes   No
     or action.

20. I like the strong feelings that come with my   Yes   No
     anger.

21. Sometimes when I am bored I start arguments   Yes   No
     or pick fights.

- -

22. I seem to get angry all the time.   Yes   No

23. My anger feels like a bad habit I have trouble   Yes   No
     breaking.

24. I get mad without thinking—it feels automatic.   Yes   No

- -

25. I get jealous a lot, even when there is no reason.   Yes   No

26. I don't trust people very much.   Yes   No

27. Sometimes it feels like people are out to get me.   Yes   No

- -

28. I become very angry when I defend my beliefs   Yes   No
     and opinions.

29. I often feel outraged about what others try to   Yes   No
     get away with.

30. I always know I'm right in an argument.   Yes   No

- -

31. I hang onto my anger for a long time.   Yes   No

32. I have a hard time forgiving people.   Yes   No

33. I hate people for what they've done to me.   Yes   No

Notice that the questions are broken into sets of three. Each set is about one special anger style.

If you have one Yes answer in a set of three questions, you'll want to read about that style. If you have two Yes answers, that style is one of your favorites. It's affecting you a lot, so read about it very carefully. And if you have three Yes answers, you've hit the jackpot. That is an anger style you use frequently, maybe all the time. It's not just a style but a way of life that may be causing you problems.

Let's name the eleven anger styles and say a few words about each.

Questions 1–3: Anger Avoidance

Sally says she'll meet Joe for lunch. But she doesn't show up. It's the third time in a row, but is Joe angry? Of course not. He never gets mad, he says. Joe would feel like a bad person if he got angry.

Anger avoiders don't like anger much. Some avoiders are afraid of their anger, or the anger of others. Anger seems too scary to touch. They're scared of losing control if they get mad, of letting out the monster inside them. Other avoiders think that it's bad to be angry. They've learned sayings like "Only dogs get mad" and "Be nice, don't be angry." They hide from their anger because they want to be liked.

Anger avoiders gain the sense of being a good or nice person because they don't get mad. That helps them feel safe and calm.

Anger avoiders have problems, though. They often don't feel anger even when something is wrong, so anger doesn't help them survive. Also, they can't be assertive, because they feel too guilty when they say what they want. Too often the result is that they are walked over by others.

Questions 4–6: Sneaky Anger

The church ladies are calling again. They want Ruth to make sandwiches for 100 people next week at the social. Ruth has other plans, but she says okay. The day of the picnic comes, and no Ruth.

She just forgot, she explains when they call, and now there isn't time. Too bad, but they'll have to do something else.

Anger sneaks never let others know they are angry. In fact, sometimes they don't even know how angry they are. But the anger comes out "sideways" when they forget things a lot, or say "Yeah, but . . ." over and over instead of doing anything, or when they simply sit around and frustrate everybody in their families. When others get mad at them, anger sneaks can look hurt and innocent. "Why are you getting mad at me?" they ask. "I haven't done anything." And that's the problem. Because they are angry, anger sneaks don't do what they are asked or told to do, but they don't tell anybody about their resentments.

Anger sneaks gain a sense of control over their lives when they frustrate others. By doing little or nothing, or by putting things off, they thwart other people's plans. In addition, they can be angry without having to admit it. "It's not my fault you expect too much from me," they say.

Sneaky anger creates problems, though. The biggest one is that anger sneaks lose track of their own wants and needs. True, they can keep from meeting the demands of others, but then what? They don't know what they want to do with their lives. That leads to boredom, frustration, and unsatisfying relationships.

Questions 7–9: Anger Turned Inward

Judy is angry at her husband Rick because he stayed out drinking again last night, not coming home until 3 A.M. She'd like to tell him off the next morning but she doesn't say a word. Instead, she gets angry at herself. "It's all my fault," she thinks. "If I were a better wife, Rick would want to stay home with me." Judy calls herself names a lot, blames herself for anything that goes wrong in her family's life, and even occasionally pinches her arm as a form of self-punishment.

Judy has turned most of her anger onto herself. She does this because she learned early on that she was a safer target for her anger than anybody else. Getting angry with herself keeps her from rocking the boat. Besides, she truly believes that expressing her anger out loud won't be useful. The last time she did that Rick got real angry back at her, and she felt too scared to stand her ground.

Anger turned inward can be helpful. It's important for each of us to ask ourselves if we have done anything wrong in a situation and sometimes to get mad enough at ourselves to change our behavior. Too much anger turned inward, though, can increase a person's feelings of helplessness and hopelessness.

Questions 10–12: Sudden Anger

Martha is furious. Her mother expects her to move out of the house some day. How dare she! Martha's instantly enraged. She's yelling and throwing things, beating her fists on the wall. Her rage only lasts a few minutes, but by then her mom is crying and running out the door.

People with sudden anger are like thunderstorms on a summer day. They zoom in from nowhere, blast everything in sight, and then vanish. Sometimes it's only thunder and lightning, a big show that soon blows away. But often people get hurt, homes are broken up, and things are damaged that will take a long time to repair.

People with sudden anger gain a surge of power. They release all their feelings, so they feel good or relieved. They "let it all hang out," for better or worse.

Loss of control is a major problem with sudden anger. People with sudden anger can be dangerous to themselves and others. They may get violent. They say and do things they later regret, but by then it's too late to take them back.

Questions 13–15: Shame-based Anger

Mary's husband Bill drives over to pick her up. When he gets there he forgets to ask her how she enjoyed the movie. "Well, that's proof he doesn't love me," she thinks to herself. "If he cared, he'd want to know about my day. Boy, does that burn me up!"

People who need a lot of attention or are very sensitive to criticism often develop this anger style. The slightest criticism sets off their own shame. Unfortunately, they don't like themselves very much. They feel worthless, not good enough, broken, unlovable. So when somebody ignores them or says something negative, they take it as proof that the other person dislikes them as much as they dislike themselves. But that gets them really angry, so they lash out. They think: "You made me feel awful, so I'm gonna hurt you back."

People with this anger style play hot potato with their shame. They get rid of their shame by blaming, criticizing, and ridiculing others. Their anger helps them get revenge against anybody they think shamed them. They avoid their own feelings of inadequacy by shaming others.

Raging against others to hide shame doesn't work very well. Those with shame-based anger end up attacking the people they love. Meanwhile, they continue to be oversensitive to insults because of their poor self-image. Their anger and loss of control only makes them feel worse about themselves.

Questions 16–18: Deliberate Anger

William wants sex tonight. His wife says no. He starts to pout, and then accuses her of being cold. He looks awfully angry, almost out of control. Odd, though, that when his wife gives in and says she'll go to bed with him, his anger vanishes. How can someone be terribly angry one second and totally calm the next?

Deliberate anger is planned. People who use anger this way usually know what they are doing. They aren't really emotional about their anger, at least not at first. They like controlling others, and the best way they've discovered to do that is with anger and, sometimes, violence.

Power and control are what people gain from deliberate anger. Their goal is to get what they want by threatening or overpowering others.

Deliberate anger may work for a while. However, this style usually breaks down in the long run. People don't like to be bullied, and eventually they figure out ways to escape or get back at the bully.

Questions 19–21: Excitatory Anger

Melinda feels depressed a lot, bored with her life. But once in a while she gets bent out of shape and really blows up. "You know what," she told us, "I really feel alive when I get into a fight. That adrenaline rush is great. That's the only time I feel excited."

Some people want or need the strong feelings that come with anger. They like the intensity even if they don't like the trouble their anger causes them. Their anger is much more than a bad habit—it provides emotional excitement. Anger isn't fun, but it is powerful. Rageaholics look forward to the anger "rush," the emotional "high." These people will have trouble giving up their anger. Like those who cling to gambling, cocaine, or risk-taking behaviors, their lives seem dull without these periods of tremendous feeling. They gain a surge of intensity and emotional power when they explode. They feel alive and full of energy.

This pattern of excitement seeking can become painful and damaging. People can become dependent upon their anger to feel good. Then they pick fights just to get high on anger. And, since they need intensity, their anger takes on an all-or-none pattern that creates more problems than it solves.

Questions 22–24: Habitual Hostility

Ralph is really getting tired of being angry with his kids, but he can't stop it. Every night, like clockwork, he comes home and starts screaming at them. He's angry before he even gets in the door. And when the kids give him that "Oh, there he goes again" look, he gets even angrier. Ralph has developed a hostile way of looking at the world.

Anger can become a bad habit. Habitually angry people find themselves getting angry often, usually about small things that don't bother others. They wake up grumpy. They go through the day looking for fights. They look for the worst in everything and everybody. They usually go to bed pissed off about something. They might even have angry dreams. Their angry thoughts set them up for more and more arguments. They can't seem to quit being angry, even though they are unhappy.

Habitually angry people gain predictability. They always know what they feel (because their main feeling is anger). Life may be lousy but it is known, safe, and steady.

Habitually angry people get trapped in their anger. Anger runs their lives. They can't even get close to the people they love because their anger keeps them away.

Questions 25–27: Fear-based Anger

Howard loves Millie. But he's scared he'll lose her. That's why he follows her everywhere. That's why he asks her all those questions. And he flies into a rage whenever she even glances at another man.

He's so jealous he's driving Millie crazy. She just told him that if he can't control his temper she's going to break off their relationship.

Jealousy isn't Howard's only problem. He's also suspicious a lot, often believing that others are talking about him behind his back. He doesn't trust many people, and sometimes he wonders what others are going to do next to hurt him. Frequently he accuses others of being angry or being out to "screw" him, but they usually deny it.

This is fear-based anger. It occurs when someone feels irrationally threatened by others. Those with fear-based anger see aggression everywhere. They are certain that people want to take what is theirs. They expect others will attack them physically or verbally. Because of this belief, they spend much time jealously guarding and defending what they think is theirs—the love of their partner (real or imagined), their money, or their valuables, for example.

Questions 28–30: Moral Anger

Joan is a crusader. She's always fighting for a cause. Today it's one thing, tomorrow another. But whatever it is, she's absolutely certain she is on the side of justice. She gets furious with those who think differently than she does. Joan wears the cloak of righteousness as if it were designed by her personal tailor.

Some people think they have a right to be angry when others have broken a rule. That makes the offenders bad, evil, wicked, sinful. They have to be scolded, maybe punished. They have to be brought back in line. People with this anger style feel outraged about what those bad people are doing. They say they aren't angry for themselves. They just have to fight to defend their beliefs. They claim moral superiority.

Morally angry people gain the sense that their anger is for a good cause. They don't feel guilty when they get angry because of this. Indeed, they often feel superior to others even in their anger. "Yes, I'm angry," says the crusader, "but I've got a good reason. I'm defending a good cause, so I have a right to get mad."

These people suffer from black-and-white thinking, which means they see the world too simply. They fail to understand people who are different from themselves. They often have rigid ways of thinking and doing things. Another problem with this anger style is crusading—attacking every problem or difference of opinion with moral anger when compromise or understanding might be better.

Questions 31–33: Resentment/Hate

Mona is going through the world's messiest divorce. She's on the stand now, testifying against her husband. But look at her face. You can see the hate in her eyes. She would say anything to hurt him, whether or not it's true.

Hate is hardened anger. It is a nasty anger style that happens when someone decides that at least one other person is totally evil or bad. Forgiving the other person seems impossible. Instead, the hater vows to despise the offender. Hate starts as anger that doesn't get resolved. Then it becomes a resentment, and then a true hatred that can go on indefinitely. Haters often think about ways they can punish the offender, and sometimes they act on those ideas.

People who hate gain the feeling that they are innocent victims. They create a world of enemies to fight, and they attack them with great vigor and enthusiasm.

However, hatred causes serious damage over time. Haters can't let go or get on with life. They become bitter and frustrated. Their lives become mean, small, and narrow.

Not all resentments become hatreds, though. Many times people just stew over past injuries and offenses, feeling hurt and wounded but still maintaining some sense of perspective on the situation. Still, resentments contribute to feelings of depression, despair, and misery. This anger style, like all the others, can become problematic when it becomes habitual.

GROUPING THE STYLES

Each of these eleven styles is different from the rest. However, they form three main groups: masked anger, explosive anger, and chronic anger.

The first group (questions 1–9) is *masked* anger. Anger is masked when people don't realize that they are angry, or when they severely underestimate their anger. Anger avoidance is a mask worn so tightly that it's hard to get off. Anger avoiders try never to see their anger at all, and never to let others see it either. Sneaky anger also fits here. Those with sneaky anger hide their feelings behind masks of confusion, procrastination, and laziness. Anger turned inward is the third masked style. Here the problem is not so much that people don't realize how angry they are. Rather, they cannot give themselves permission to express their anger outwardly toward others.

The second group (questions 10–21) is *explosive* anger. People with explosive anger are known by the quick, exaggerated, and sometimes dangerous character of their anger. Obviously, sudden anger is an explosive style, since it is marked by loss of control and quick rages; but so is shame-based anger. Shame-prone people often feel suddenly attacked, and they lash out defensively in return. Deliberate anger is another explosive style. Those who get angry intentionally have to demonstrate that they will "go crazy" to get what they want. We also include excitatory anger as an explosive style. People who frequently become angry in this way seek an adrenaline rush. They achieve that kind of high when they get into loud and energetic arguments.

The third group (questions 22–33) is *chronic* anger. Those with this style stew in their anger for long periods. They can't let go of their anger as easily as those with any of the other styles. Habitual anger is one chronic style. Here people have learned the habit of anger so well they can't stop. Fear-based anger makes people distrustful and even paranoid. Those who hate are stuck in an anger that won't release them. And people with moral anger get locked into endless crusades. They can fight forever but can't figure out how to quit.

Do you see yourself in one or more of these styles? If so, keep going. We have arranged the chapters by groups, beginning with the masked anger styles, then the explosive ones, and finally the chronic anger styles. You don't have to read the chapters in order. But make sure to look at the next section, on healthy anger, either now, or somewhere along the line.

ANGER, ANGER STYLES, AND FLEXIBILITY

Anger is an important emotion. Just like the other "primary" emotions such as fear, sadness, disgust, and happiness, anger is an emotional messenger. The message of anger is this: "Hey, something is going wrong here. Something's blocking my path. Do something about it." Actually, anger serves two main purposes: it tells you there is something significantly wrong and it gives you the energy to attempt to change things.

Anger has its limits, though. It gives you a message. It gives you energy. But anger cannot tell you exactly how to handle any situation. Essentially, anger says, "Do something to get that boulder out of my path." But it cannot make specific plans like "Here's how. Get some dynamite and blow it up" or "Ask your buddies to help roll it off the path" or even "Ignore that boulder. Just walk around it."

That's where the idea of anger styles fits in. An "anger style" is a predictable, repeated way to handle situations in which you are or could become angry. Essentially each anger style directs you into handling your anger in a slightly different manner. Each anger style is like a personal guide on your path of life, telling you one good way to deal with frustrations, obstacles, and annoyances. The only problem is that each guide is a creature of habit, giving you the same advice over and over. One guide, in the voice of anger avoidance, pretty much always says, "Don't disturb that boulder. Maybe it will go away if we don't push on it." Another guide, in the voice of moral anger, says, "That boulder has no right to be blocking my path. Let's make it feel guilty." A third, in the voice of sudden anger, says, "Let's blast it right now with dynamite before we even try to think of another way." But which guide should you listen to? How should you handle your anger? What will you do about that boulder?

That's where you need to be flexible. The fact is there are many different ways to express anger. No way is always right or wrong. Flexibility is a key to well-being in the area of anger management. Can you select from all the available options (the eleven styles) the best choice for a particular situation? For example, anger avoidance may be perfectly sensible in many situations where it's just not worth the effort to get into a battle. But it would be disastrous to choose anger avoidance in other situations—for instance, if you discover your work buddy is showing up at work every day spaced-out on cocaine.

Rigidity is the opposite of flexibility. With anger, being rigid means always choosing one or two styles no matter what the circumstances. The old saying "If the only tool you have is a hammer, then every problem becomes a nail" reflects the limits of someone who uses only one or two anger styles to handle every situation.

Fortunately, most people use more than one style, depending on the situations they are in. Still, we humans are indeed creatures of habit. That means we tend to favor the particular anger styles that we use most frequently. The styles that we prefer are usually the ones we were taught as children. Basically, each of us has learned that it is better to handle our anger in certain ways than others.

Each anger style has value when used wisely. On the other hand, any anger style can be overused, poorly used, or misused—creating problems. Hopefully, by reading this book, you will be able to better decide which anger style to use in different situations. The idea is to have many tools in your toolkit and to know when and how to use each of them.

HEALTHY ANGER

Anger is a tricky emotion, difficult to use well until you learn how. It is a real help, though, as long as you don't get trapped in any of the anger styles we've introduced here. People who use anger well have a healthy or "normal" relationship with their anger. They think about anger in the following characteristic ways:

- Anger is treated as a normal part of life.

- Anger is an accurate signal of real problems in a person's life.

- Angry actions are screened carefully; you needn't automatically get angry just because you could.

- Anger is expressed in moderation so there is no loss of control.

- The goal is to solve problems, not just to express anger.

- Anger is clearly stated in ways that others can understand.

- Anger is temporary. It can be relinquished once an issue is resolved.

You can learn to handle your anger well. First, recognize that anger is a normal part of life. Everybody feels angry from time to time. Like all feelings, anger is neither good nor bad, it just is.

When you are comfortable with yourself you don't hide from your anger. Nor is anger your best friend. Rather, accept your anger for what it is: a signal that something is wrong in your life. Anger acts like a blinking light at a railroad crossing. It only goes on once in a while, but when it does there really is a train coming down the tracks. Anger tells you to look for the problem. It also tells you to do something to make the situation better.

Another important idea about healthy anger is the ability to screen *anger invitations.* Every day you get many chances to become angry. For instance, a driver cuts in front of your car on the way to work. Someone else criticizes you. Another person doesn't return your call. All these are anger invitations. You could accept every one, in which case you'll be angry all the time.

Instead, you have to be careful. The key is to ignore the less important invitations. You have to separate what is merely annoying from what is really serious.

When you do get angry, express anger in moderation. Learning how to tell others about your anger without losing control is a vital part of healthy anger. There is a big difference between telling others you're angry and screaming at them. People get defensive when you yell. They scream back. They quit listening.

Handling anger well also means that the goal is to solve problems, not hurt others. You are angry with someone because of a conflict. Between you there is a shortage of time, money, love, power, or something else important. You want something from them. They want something from you. You're angry because it's frustrating to have conflict. But that's life. The job is to find a way to get what you want, without hurting others.

You can learn effective ways to communicate your anger and what you want. One way is to tell others specifically what is bothering you. Use "I messages," which go like this:

When you _____ *(specific behavior)* _____ ,

I feel _____ *(specific feeling)* _____ ,

and I want _____ *(specific goal)* _____ .

For instance: "Joe, when you say you'll be home at nine o'clock and don't get home until midnight, I get worried and angry, and I want you to call by ten if you're delayed."

Or: "Jessica, when you swear at me and call me stupid, I get defensive and hurt, and I want you to quit swearing and not to call me stupid. I want you to quit shouting, too, and sit down when we are talking."

When you practice good anger skills you never need to use your anger as an excuse. You can take responsibility for what you say and do, even when you are mad.

A final measure of healthy anger is the ability to let it go once it has served its purpose. It's easy to hang onto anger, of course. But what good does it do when the problem is over? Let that anger fade, so you can get on with life.

We will describe all eleven anger styles in the rest of the book. Please bear in mind that probably no one uses only one style each and every time he or she feels angry. As you read through the chapters, try asking yourself these questions:

- In general, which of these styles do I use quite frequently?

- In general, which of the styles do I avoid?

- Do I use different styles with different people or in different situations? For example, some people might practice sudden anger more often at home than at work where they are more likely to be anger avoiders. If so, why?

- When do I use any particular style well? How do I use it well?

- When do I use any particular style poorly? How do I use it poorly?

- How flexible or rigid am I in the styles I use to handle my anger?

- How could I become better at handling my anger?

II

Masked Anger Styles

2

Anger Avoidance

Run! Get away fast! Danger ahead! A monster's on the loose!

The name of the monster is Anger.

Anger avoiders are scared of their anger. They don't like the feeling at all. Anger feels bad, dangerous, nasty, ugly. Anger is not a friend of theirs. In fact, they view anger as an enemy, something to avoid at all costs.

What, exactly, are they so scared of? Lots of things, such as:

- *Loss of control.* "Ron, you don't understand. I hate my anger. It's so powerful. I'm afraid if I ever let it out I will go completely nuts. Maybe I'll kill somebody, or go crazy. Sure, you can be a little angry, but not me. I've got to hide from my anger or it will ruin me. I feel like I'll destroy the world if I get angry."

- *Rejection.* "Pat, my family scolds me when I get mad. Why, a couple days ago I complained that the kids got home late. I don't think I raised my voice. But they told me I was awful, and my husband wouldn't talk to me for the rest of the night. I don't get angry anymore because I can't stand the rejection."

- *Punishment.* "My father was a terrible man. He beat us up. I didn't dare get mad back because when I did he hit me more. I learned never to show my anger to anyone."

- *Getting stuck in the anger.* "Sure, I could get angry. But I'm afraid I won't be able to stop once I get started. So I stop myself first. I don't want to be a rageaholic like my mother."

- *Guilt.* "I was taught that anger is a weakness. Good people *never* get mad. Period. I feel guilty if I even start getting upset. So I don't let anything bother me, and I refuse to tell anyone I'm angry with them."

Some people treat their anger as if it were their appendix—a useless organ that can only cause trouble. To them, anger is outdated, something from the Stone Age. It's not nice to be angry. It's dumb to get mad. Good people just don't let themselves get upset, and if they do, they certainly don't tell anyone. They can be good, or angry. They cannot be both good and angry. Or so they think.

Anger avoiders squirm uncomfortably when they have to face their anger, like ten-year-olds who have been told by their parents to go over and talk to each other at a party: "Do I have to? I don't wanna. I won't know what to say. I wanna stay over here with my friends." They really would prefer never to be introduced. And if avoiders are forced to meet their anger, they try to get away fast. Any excuse will do. Who wants to spend time with that stinky old feeling anyhow?

Anger avoiders also don't like to meet other people's anger. "Yuck," they say to themselves. "Why would you want to spend time with anybody's anger? I don't like my anger. I don't like your anger. I don't like their anger. If anger's been invited to the party, then I'm staying home, thank you." Other people's anger scares them and turns them off. They don't want any part of it, no matter how important the situation. We wrote in chapter 1 about the value of anger as a messenger. It tells you, and others, that something is wrong. If you pay attention to that message, maybe you can figure out what you can do to change things. The trouble is that anger avoiders are too scared of anger to listen to the message. They run away or pretend that there is no problem rather than notice the messenger.

Maybe the message is that your boss is treating you like dirt. Or your body needs sleep and you've been ignoring it. Or your kids are taking advantage of you. Or your spouse is unfaithful. No matter. You have no intention of taking in any information if anger is the message. If you're lucky the messenger will go away after a while and you'll be able to relax. Of course, your boss will keep throwing dirt on you, your body will fall apart, your kids will throw drug parties while you're gone, and your spouse will keep sneaking out of the house at midnight. But who cares? At least you didn't get angry. You are an excellent anger avoider.

Anger avoidance is the first anger style we discuss because it's so common in American society. That's because our society is pretty scared of anger, and it is becoming more so as violence increases throughout the world. Americans see anger as a problem. Anger disrupts the smooth flow of life. It threatens law and order. Anger causes trouble. In many subtle ways we are told, over and over, to hold in our anger. Be nice, no matter what. Get angry and you could lose your reputation, your marriage, your friends, your job.

So we learn to ignore our anger. Instead of recognizing it as a part of being human, we try to throw it away. We disown our anger. "Anger, get out of my life. Remove yourself from my mind. Stay away from my body. I refuse to get angry. You are bad, bad, bad."

This is a waste. Anger is not an enemy. It is part of me, and you, and everybody. It is a fact of life. Avoiding anger means losing something important, something that could make life a lot happier.

THE VALUE OF ANGER AVOIDANCE

Every anger style has its uses. That is certainly very true for anger avoidance. Here are several positive aspects of anger avoidance:

- *Anger avoidance helps you to be more selective.* People are frequently offered what we call "anger invitations." These invitations are basically everything that happens that is at least slightly annoying: the guy who cuts ahead of you on the street or in a line; the too cold coffee or too warm can of soda; the discovery that your spouse is having an affair. Most people realize fairly early in life that they better say "No thank you" to most anger invitations or they will spend way too much time being angry. But it is also important to say, "Yes, I will let myself get angry" some of the time.

■ *Anger avoidance saves energy.* Becoming angry takes time, effort, and energy that might better be used in other activities. When someone says, "Sure, I could get mad about that but it's not worth the trouble," that person is conserving energy.

■ *Anger avoidance could save your life.* Anger begets anger, so your anger may trigger someone else's anger. That, in turn, could lead to arguments, aggression, and violence. Walking away from your anger may keep you safe.

■ *Anger avoidance may be socially rewarded while expressing anger is punished.* We often praise children for not getting into fights, for being nice and polite, for controlling their emotions. At the same time we punish children, especially girls, for getting angry. Guilt and shame are used to reinforce anger avoidance. No wonder some children grow into adults who deny their own anger to themselves and seldom express anger out loud.

■ *Anger avoidance buys time.* Sometimes it's best to take a day or two to think through an issue before expressing one's anger. Buying time gives you space to think about the problem, come up with ideas on how to resolve it, and perhaps most importantly to gain a sense of perspective: "You know, when I first heard I wasn't invited to that party I started to get mad. I almost picked up the phone to tell off the host. But I slept on it and the next day realized I had told her I probably would be out of town the day of the party. I'm glad I kept my mouth shut."

So anger avoidance definitely has value. It's an important tool to keep in your anger management toolbox. However, anger avoidance becomes a problem when people too frequently avoid feeling or expressing their anger. Serious issues usually don't go away just by ignoring them. They must be faced.

HOW ANGER AVOIDERS HIDE FROM THEIR ANGER

For many people, a day without pain is a good day. For anger avoiders, a good day's a day without anger. Anger is pain, and fear, and guilt. Anger is bad. Anger is the enemy. How do anger avoiders fight the enemy? With a special set of tools.

Imagine that people with a particular anger style have a toolbox with a set of special tools. Exploders, for instance, may have a balloon that quickly inflates and then makes a lot of noise when it blows. Haters have super glue that helps them stay stuck to their anger for years. People with a deliberate anger style have a calendar for marking down the best times to get pissed off.

Anger avoiders have their own tools. The first is a perfectly fitted *blindfold*. That's so they can deny that there's any reason to get angry. It's actually a double blindfold. It keeps them from seeing anything to get mad about and also keeps them from noticing any signs of their body's anger. True, their hands keep folding into fists, but avoiders just ignore them. Maybe they'll go away. *Earplugs* are a must, too. Anger avoiders don't want to hear any upsetting news. No news is good news, and no anger means nothing to worry about.

The next tool is a *mute*, the kind trumpeters use to play softer. That's to tone down any anger that does break through. "Who me, angry? Well, I guess a little bit, maybe, but just a smidgen. No sense getting really mad, is there?" The mute minimizes anger, so it never gets loud enough to bother anyone. Anger avoiders try to make sure their anger only whispers at them. They don't like it when it gets too loud.

Anger avoiders often carry a *shield*, like the one used by the Enterprise on *Star Trek* to deflect enemy missiles. Anger avoiders fear their anger will hurt them or others, so they dodge it whenever they can.

A large *spinner* is essential. This is useful when anger avoiders begin to get bothered. They jump on the spinner until they become dizzy and totally confused. "Gee, I don't know what I'm feeling. I guess I'm angry, but maybe not. I can't figure anything out anymore." When they stay confused they don't have to do anything.

A *doormat* helps, too. That's so anger avoiders have something to lie on when others stomp all over them. People who can't use anger to defend themselves often become victims, taken advantage of by others who are less afraid of aggression.

THE COSTS OF ANGER AVOIDANCE

You pay a huge price when you ignore your anger. It's the same as not fixing a big hole in the roof of your home. Perhaps you see it there, but you're too busy to do anything. It may not rain or snow for a few days, but sooner or later it will, and then you'll have to pay for all the damage done inside. And you'll still have a hole in your roof, waiting for the next storm.

Avoiding anger takes a heavy toll on your personal well-being. If you are an anger avoider your losses range from not getting what you want to suffering physical illness and depression.

Not Getting What You Want

Anger tells you that you aren't getting something you want. Maybe it's a day off from work, or money to buy some new clothes. Maybe it's being treated decently by your partner. But anger can't say much when you are wearing earplugs.

Avoiding your anger causes frustration. Like a squirrel that spent all summer gathering food, only to forget where he put it come winter, you "stuff" your anger and forget how to take care of yourself. Without your anger all you can say is "Oh, no, I don't need any time off. I'll be happy to work twelve days in a row." Or: "No, honey, it's fine that you bought yourself those $100 tennis shoes. I guess I didn't need a new suit anyhow."

Anger avoiders lose their voice. Without it, they are doomed to sit silently while others get their way.

Loss of Part of Yourself

Anger avoiders have found a perfect way not to make fists. Unfortunately, their solution is to cut off their hands. They don't reach for what they want or need because they might provoke someone. They can't change things in the world to fit them better because they have given up so much of their power. Now they have to depend upon others, or run away.

Anger is part of all human beings. We aren't complete without it. So when people become anger avoiders they destroy a big part of themselves. They are no longer whole.

Most anger avoiders know something is wrong. They don't feel very good about themselves. They call themselves names like "doormat," "weakling," "stupid," even "codependent." They've lost their self-respect. But often they can't quite figure out what's wrong. If anything, they try to be even nicer, always less angry. That's their style. That's how they solve life's problems. If that means cutting off their hands to avoid making fists, so be it. If that's not enough, well, then, maybe it's necessary to lop off their feet to keep from kicking up a fuss.

Turning the Anger Against Yourself

Terry was so mad at Marvin she wanted to poke his eyes out. Instead, she scratched and scratched her arm until she drew blood.

Jeff never gets mad at others. But not a day goes by that he doesn't insult himself out loud. "I'm such an idiot!" he tells everybody. "I'm nothing but an ugly loser." And he believes it.

These two anger avoiders have turned their natural anger toward others onto themselves. All the anger, fair or unfair, that they could feel toward others has been redirected, like a boomerang that smacks the person who threw it on the back of her own head.

Why do this? Because these anger avoiders think it's safer to hurt themselves than others. They would rather punch themselves in the stomach in utter frustration than say, "I'm mad at you." They would rather feel bad about themselves than risk losing others. So some anger avoiders become self-abusers, punishing themselves over and over with the anger that really is meant for others.

Depression and Physical Illness

Anger avoiders often develop physical and emotional illnesses. They can get depressed, not only because depression is "anger turned inward" (actually, we think self-hatred is a better term for that kind of anger), but mostly because anger avoiders feel so helpless and hopeless. Without anger, they can't get what they want or do what they need to do. That's when they get depressed. Almost anyone would, if they were too afraid of their anger to use it well.

Anger avoiders also get headaches, ulcers, nervous conditions, allergic reactions, and lots of other partly psychologically caused sicknesses. They may eat too much to stuff down their anger, drink too much trying to forget it, or spend too much hoping to make themselves happy.

Stuff and Blow

Anger avoiders will do anything to escape from their anger. But it follows them like a large, stealthy cat silently tracking them down, waiting to pounce.

Finally, the cat springs, often without warning. One moment the anger avoider is just sitting there, ignoring her anger as usual. The next, she's a raging tiger, screaming insanely over and over, "I can't stand it anymore. I won't take it. I'm so mad I could kill." The anger finally breaks through, and now there's hell to pay for all those hours, and days, and weeks, and months, that it's been stuffed so deep inside. This anger comes out as rage—irrational, exaggerated, and dangerous.

Later, she'll feel incredibly guilty. "How could I do that?" she'll moan. How could she, such a nice and gentle woman, swear her head off at her husband and kids? How could she have thrown the spaghetti on the wall and the poodle out the window? How could she have told them she was going to pack that night and never come home? Oh, the looks on their faces! She wonders if they'll ever forgive her. She can't believe she'll be able to forgive herself, either.

She swears that she will never do that again. Never. She doesn't notice the cat in the background, again ready to pounce on her with all that anger.

HAVE YOU HAD ENOUGH OF YOUR NICE GUY?

He's sweet as chocolate milk, as friendly as a newborn puppy, as pure as a baby's smile. He's cute. He's cuddly.

And he's gotta go!

That adorable, childlike nice guy of yours, the one who just wants to be loved, is wrecking your life. Mr. Nice Guy is your anger avoider. He's the one afraid to say "boo" on Halloween. He's the one who tries to convince you that anger is bad, or dangerous, or both. He's like gum stuck to your shoe, and you're going to have to find a stick to scrape him off.

Change begins with a vision of the future. Before we go on, we suggest you take a few minutes to picture yourself in an altered state. Imagine your nice guy is on a well-earned vacation. For once in your life you can really be angry. You can get mad, stay mad, and use your anger well. Here are a few things that you might envision:

- See yourself calmly and firmly insisting on being treated with respect by someone who often takes you for granted or is abusive to you.

- Think about how you would look as you get angry. How do you stand? What happens to your eyes and mouth? Does your voice rise or fall?

- Imagine using your anger well, and then feel the satisfaction. Notice the rise in self-respect. Feel your pride and confidence grow. At last you can defend and speak up for yourself.

- Let yourself feel the very first hints of your anger: stomach twinges, a vague sense of irritation, a slight frown or tensing of your jaw, lowering your eyebrows, tapping your foot or pacing, and so on. Those little hints are coming from the anger messenger. Paying attention to them may help you deal with a bad situation before it gets worse.

- Think of the word "no." Say no a dozen times out loud, in a dozen ways—loud, soft, fast, slow. Roll your tongue around that word as if it were the tastiest ice cream cone you ever ate. With Mr. Nice Guy on vacation, you can add no to your vocabulary.

All this may be a little scary at first. But don't let the fear paralyze you. It's just your avoider trying to keep you out of trouble. Probably that was helpful to you in the past. Then you needed your anger avoider because it really was too dangerous to get angry. Today, we hope, things are different. (If they aren't, you need to examine your situation carefully. Maybe you need to make some major changes if you cannot safely listen to or act upon your anger.) Realistically, you can let yourself get angry from time to time. It won't turn you or others into monsters.

The next step toward change is to make a commitment. No more nice guy. No more doormat. No more dread of anger. From now on anger has a place in your life. You can be real at last. You can be whole.

We're not suggesting that you should be angry all the time. That would be going from one extreme to the other. What's important is that you can notice and use your anger well when it's needed.

Anger avoiders are trapped by a rigid rule: Never get angry, no matter what. This rule allows no exceptions. A person who is angry is always bad or wrong.

Maybe that rule was useful before. Perhaps you had no choice but to follow it. But it's outdated now, like the food left too long on the grocer's shelf. It's time to change that rule.

The anger avoider's pledge: Beginning today, I will allow anger to be part of my family of emotions. Anger has a place in my life, along with sadness, joy, and all my other feelings. I promise to listen to my anger, to use it to help me figure out what to say or do, and to let go of my anger when the situation is better.

USE YOUR ANGER WELL

Anger is a strong feeling that takes a lot of energy. It's also easy to waste or misuse. Endless nagging, insisting that something change that can't be altered, refusing to let go of anger when things do change, and complaining for the sake of complaining are all ways to waste anger. Anger avoiders who are just learning to accept their anger need to make sure they use their anger well.

Here are three tips for the good use of anger:

Be sure the thing you feel angry about is important, not a mere annoyance. For example, your employer gives everybody in the office but you a raise. Something's sure wrong here. Your anger tells you to find out what's happening, and why.

Tell the person you're angry with exactly what you want. "Sally, I want you to call me by half past ten if you're not going to be home by midnight." That doesn't mean you'll always get what you want, of course. But this way you know specifically what you are fighting for.

Stick with your anger. You may be inclined to let go of your anger too soon. The fear or guilt creeps in and you feel anxious or sick. Or you simply give up, convinced you'll never get what you want or need.

Mary, an anger avoider, has "tolerated" her husband George's affairs for years. Finally she confronts him with clear proof of his womanizing. George quickly admits it, then begs Mary to forgive him for being a bad boy. Her heart goes out to him. How can she stay mad at him when he sounds so sincere? The poor boy.

Yes, he's wonderful. But he's also suckered her again. Where's the promise to stay faithful? Where's the immediate call or letter to the woman he's involved with calling it off?

You have to stay angry long enough to make sure something good happens. Hang in there, despite the fear and the guilt. Don't let your nice guy sabotage you just when you are getting somewhere.

LET OTHERS BE ANGRY

Anger avoiders have to learn that it's okay for people to get angry once in a while. They don't have to try to quiet down their partners all the time, to hush up their children, to smooth over things at work, to keep everybody happy. That's not their job.

We've raised three children into adulthood. Like all kids, sometimes they got into arguments with each other. As parents, it was our job to let them argue, as long as they fought fair and didn't hit. We'd step in when we had to. But not every time. They had to learn to speak up for themselves, both inside and outside the family.

Anger avoiders often come from families in which normal anger was not permitted. Their parents would stop them at the first hint of a fight. "Everybody be nice" was the order. No wonder they grew up so uncomfortable with anger.

Anger does not destroy relationships—not when it's handled well, as part of the natural order of things, as a signal that something is wrong and needs immediate attention. In fact, avoidance often does more damage to partnerships, families, and friendships than expression of anger. Things left unsaid are like ghosts. They'll haunt the household until they are dealt with honestly and openly.

If you're an anger avoider, take a deep breath the next time someone in your family gets angry. Don't rush to make things nice. Don't intervene unless there is real danger.

What if someone gets mad at you? Well, don't accept abuse. But don't do something you don't really want to do just to make them happy right away, either. Pay attention to their anger. Ask yourself what it's about. Does the person who is angry at you have a good reason? If so, do what you can to fix things. If you honestly think they are wrong, explain your position. Don't back down just to make peace.

GETTING BEYOND ANGER AVOIDANCE

We suggest you sign up for an assertiveness training class if you are an anger avoider. Assertiveness training teaches the differences among assertive, passive, and aggressive behaviors. It will help you express your anger in ways that don't hurt others. Still, anger avoiders could take a hundred assertiveness classes and not change a bit. Those who cannot change still believe that their anger is bad.

Anger avoidance is an anger style, a habitual way of thinking and acting. Anger avoiders answer the question "what do I do with my anger?" by saying "I won't have it." That strategy sometimes works. What you don't notice may go away. Too often, though, anger avoiders don't deal with reality. They don't hear the important messages their anger tries to deliver. And so their lives get worse.

Anger avoiders can and do change, though. They learn to accept four main ideas:

- Anger is normal.

- I can be angry.

- I am a good person even when angry.

- I can use my anger well.

Examine these four ideas for yourself now.

Anger Is Normal

Having the feeling called anger is a normal, human event. But how people express their feeling of anger differs. You may know (or have known) someone who expresses anger in loud, mean, or controlling ways. Being noisy or mean is different from having a feeling. Take some time now to think about what is different about having a feeling and taking an action. Ask yourself, "Who taught me that anger was bad?" Then ask yourself, "Who showed me a kind of angry behavior I didn't want to have?" Now ask yourself, "Who do I know who shows me that having a feeling of anger is normal, and different from losing control or hurting other people?"

I Can Be Angry

Start to listen more to the messages that your body sends you. For example, when you have a knot in your shoulder or your stomach, ask yourself what is happening that you do *not* like. Try putting that knot into your fist instead. Do you feel any less afraid? That is your anger defending you. Ask what it wants to say. When your jaw muscles get tight, ask yourself, "If I were angry now, what would I want to say?" When you catch yourself slamming a door, heaving a big sigh of hopelessness, or working hard to get rid of excess energy, let yourself notice that you can be angry. Ask yourself if you are, in fact, angry right then. You can still choose what to do about your anger. But honor the feeling itself. It is there to help you when something in your world is out of balance.

I Am a Good Person Even When Angry

Giving and taking need to be balanced in life. Everyone needs space, respect, and the opportunity to do something for themselves. Everyone also needs to have boundaries for physical and emotional safety. Anger is the energy that helps you achieve a balance between giving and taking, and helps you set these healthy boundaries for yourself. Anger itself is not selfish or harmful. If you are a person who feels guilty whenever you feel angry, you have learned a rigid way of thinking. Anger can be good if you use it well. Next time you feel bad about getting angry, put your arms around yourself, give yourself an actual hug, and remind yourself that you are all right, and everyone needs to be their own best friend sometimes. Tell yourself that right now is a good time for you to be your own best friend, and it is good to be angry when bad things are happening.

I Can Use My Anger Well

Remember that there is a difference between a feeling and a behavior. Our friend Charles Rumberg always says, "Feel the feeling. Choose the behavior." Make a list of behaviors that you would approve of in a friend who needed to get some respect, stand up for himself, or get help when he was doing too much of the work. Carry that list of behaviors to use for yourself, when you find yourself feeling angry. Ask a friend who expresses himself in a way you respect about other behaviors you could add to your list. Try them out. Using your anger well means that you request clearly what you want, insist on getting at least some of what you need, don't call names or physically harm another person, and stand up for yourself if you feel pushed around by others.

3

Sneaky Anger

The basic question we're asking in this book is this: How do people handle their anger? Each anger style gives a different answer. The avoider, for instance, tries never to get angry in the first place.

Anger sneaks (known more formally as passive aggressors) have their own answer: *I'll only show my anger indirectly. You'll know I'm angry by what I don't do.*

This is very clever. Anger sneaks can be angry without ever having to admit it. They never attack directly. They can't be accused of aggression. They can honestly say, "I don't understand why you're so upset. I haven't done anything." And they haven't, either. They haven't mowed the grass as they said they would (you were almost certain they promised, but maybe they didn't; you can't be 100 percent sure). They haven't filled out that application for work that's been sitting on the counter for weeks. They haven't suggested lovemaking for months. They haven't watched the kids so you could get a break. They haven't . . .

What's happening here? Anger sneaks are angry, sometimes very angry. They hate being ordered around. They don't like being advised, guided, or even gently directed. They want to live their own lives. They'd love to tell the whole world, "Just get off my back. I'll do what I want when I want, and you can't make me do anything." But they don't.

Anger sneaks don't say no to people. They don't say yes either. They don't say anything at all, usually, except maybe. They are masters of the art of getting people mad at them when in reality they are mad at others.

How do people get this way? Everybody has their own history, of course. But we think many anger sneaks, as children, got very mixed messages whenever they were asked to make a choice. Here's an example:

Dad: Billy, would you like to go to the ball game with me tonight?

Billy: No, Dad, I've got to study for a big test tomorrow.

Dad: Well, then, I guess you don't love me much, if you won't go to the game with me.

Next week:

Dad: Billy, want to go to the ball game tonight?

Billy: Yeah, Dad, I'll skip studying for the test so we can go together.

Dad: Well, then, I guess you're not a very serious student, are you? That sure disappoints me.

Hey, Dad, what's that kid supposed to say—Yes? No? Yes and no?

Next week:

Dad: Billy, want to go to the ball game tonight?

Billy: (silence)

Dad: Billy, answer me. Do you want to go to the game?

Billy: (silence)

Dad: Billy! Answer me, do you want to go or don't you?

Billy: Uh . . . I don't know . . . Maybe.

By now Dad's ready to strangle Billy, but Billy has finally found a way out of the trap. He couldn't say yes or no without being made to feel guilty, so he won't say anything at all. Billy's angry all right, but he would never admit it, not to Dad and probably not even to himself.

There are a lot of Billys (and Billies) walking around this planet. They are anger sneaks. Their anger comes out sideways. They have learned that silence is their best weapon.

THE ANGER SNEAK'S FAVORITE GAMES

Monopoly? Scrabble? Cards? Dungeons and Dragons? What's your choice? Almost everybody enjoys a good game once in a while.

Games have several things in common. They have ways to get started, rules to keep playing, winners and losers, and an end.

Anger sneaks play games with their anger. Let's look at a few of them.

Oops, I Forgot

The start: Someone asks you to do something. You don't want to, but of course you don't say no because then there'd be a conflict.

The rules: Say you'll do it, then don't. If reminded, get grumpy and tell them you don't need their help, you'll remember to do it all by yourself. But be sure to forget it anyhow, even if they mentioned it only a few minutes ago.

The winner: You win when people get mad at you for being so irresponsible.

The end: Others finally give up trying to get you to do anything.

The anger sneak says two things with this game. The more immediate message is "You can lead a horse to water but you can't make him drink." The long-term message is "I'll hurt you if you count on me. So don't expect anything. Quit asking."

We can give you an example. A woman we saw disliked her husband's decision to enroll in school. She didn't say much, though. Instead, she forgot to mail in his application until a day after it was due. Then she was hurt that he got upset. After all, she said, she did the best she could. How could she help it if she just happened to forget?

Yeah, But

The start: Someone wants you to do something active, such as taking a walk, going to the store, getting married, watching kids. You don't want to but there's no good reason to refuse.

The rules: You agree in principle with their suggestion: "Sure, that's a great idea." Then you remember something that stops you from doing it, something beyond your control. If they come up with a solution to that problem, outsmart them with yet another excuse. Whatever happens, don't do what they suggest. If you do, they win.

The winner: You win when they lose their temper and march off in a rage.

The end: Those stupid jerks finally give up and go for their walk alone, do their own shopping, marry someone else, and take the kids with them on the way out. Good-bye and good riddance.

Here's an example. George, a messenger, is a chronic complainer. Today his feet hurt. He wants the day off. His boss Sandy wants him to stay, though. She suggests he sit down once in a while on the route. "Yeah, but then I'll get way behind."

"Well, then," she says, "switch into more comfortable shoes."

"Oh, no," George explains, "that's against dress code."

Sandy can kiss that route good-bye. George will come up with a thousand reasons that keep him from work. None are his fault, of course.

Maybe George hates his job. Perhaps he's mad at Sandy. He'll never admit he's angry, though. It's more fun to play "yeah, but." It's safer, too. How can you fire someone for having sore feet once in a while?

I'll Do It Later

The start: Something needs to be done quickly. Others are depending on you to get it finished in time. You feel pressured and resent their pushiness. What right do they have to tell you how fast to go? You'll show them.

The rules: Use donkey tactics—the harder they push you, the slower you go. Dig in your heels. When they ask, tell them you're working on it. When they demand, complain that you're only human and you're going as fast as you can.

The winner: You win when everybody else gets all worried and excited. You're a double winner if they swear they'll never work with you again.

The end: Finally, you get it done, so nobody can accuse you of incompetence. If you've timed things just right, you'll finish just before the last, final, absolutely ultimate deadline.

Delaying tactics work well because we live in a cooperative world. If you don't get your report done, she may have to work late. When you stall on the dishes, he'll have no plates to eat dinner on. Maybe you and your spouse were planning on sex tonight. "Sorry," you say, "it just took too long to finish that phone call to Mom. You're not angry, are you?" By the way, you're sure mad at him (or her), but this is the only way you'll show it.

Playing Dumb or Helpless

"I can't put the dishes away, dear. I don't know where they go."

"I'd help you if I could, Joe, but nobody ever trained me in that procedure."

"I'm not very creative. Please don't ask me to come up with any new ideas."

Ignorance is bliss? Not often. But "ignorance means pissed" happens all the time. Anger sneaks play dumb when they're really angry that others expect them to think. Thinking, after all, is a form of work. It's something people expect or demand. And the more you think, the anger sneak believes, the more they'll expect you to think. Better to play dumb.

Anger sneaks also play helpless or incompetent. They do this a lot with critical people, but after a while it becomes a habit with everyone. The idea is to beat the critics at their own game. "If they think I'm no good, I'll show them they're right. That will really bug them."

The start: You are asked to think about or do something. You feel the pressure of people's demands, hopes, expectations. That angers you. You want them to back off, to expect less.

The rules: Act stupid. Pretend you have no brains, no intuition, no skills, no common sense, no guts, no pride, no ambition, no hope. If they say you have potential, watch out. That's just another kind of demand. Remember, you'll lose the game if you do anything well.

The winner: You win when you see the others shaking their heads in confusion. How could such a smart person act so dumb? How could he make those silly mistakes?

The end: They leave you in peace. Now you can go back to watching TV. It's better to be dumb and in control of your life than smart and trapped.

Leave Me Alone

The start: You're out in your hammock, relaxing, listening to the birds sing. Then someone shouts out the window for you to come in or wash the car or mow the lawn. Phooey! You're not gonna let them ruin your fun.

The rules: Ignore them. Pretend you didn't hear. If they come out and say something, answer, "Uh-huh, yeah, sure," but show them you're not paying any attention. If they drag you to the ball game, bring along a book to let them know you're not interested. Don't get enthusiastic about anything.

The winner: You win when they give you that look of utter frustration and go on to do things without you.

The end: Others give up on you. You hear them say things like, "Oh, don't bother to ask Dad. He's never interested in what we do."

Like all anger sneaks, those who play "leave me alone" want their independence. They feel that others take away their freedom by demanding too much sharing and joining. That angers them. They want to shove others back to protect their space. But they don't dare to say a simple no. Instead, they ignore others when they can. If that fails, they'll go along, but without joy or enthusiasm, like teenagers dragged along to their parents' dinner party. The message is this: "Sure, you can take away my freedom. But I'm in control of my energy and I won't let you have any."

You Can't Make Me

"I won't do it. I refuse. You can't make me." This anger game isn't quite as sneaky as the others. Those who play "you can't make me" take pride in being stubborn, silent, unyielding. They may not have a reason to refuse. They won't do what others want just because.

Most anger sneaks can't say yes or no very well. But this game is for those who know perfectly well how to say no. It's yes that's the big problem. Yes would mean giving in. Yes means loss of pride. Even the thought of yes is enough to make some people angry.

Children at the "terrible two's" stage and teenagers are wonderful players of "you can't make me." But some adults never outgrow their adolescence. They remain specialists in saying no forever.

The start: You are asked to do just about anything. The request may be reasonable or unfair, small or large. No matter, though. It feels like an insult to you. How dare they try to tell you what to do!

The rules: Don't give in. Be mean if necessary. They can't make you do anything. Fight them all the way. Never say yes to anything, even if you want it. That would be giving in.

The winner: You win in two possible ways. First, you get out of doing what you don't want to do. Second, and this is the sneaky part, you get some things you want without admitting it. For example, the two-year-old is "forced" to eat that ice cream cone. The teenager finally gives in to cleaning up her room (which she wants to do), but she can take pride in her defiance.

The end: Everybody gets mad and stomps off in different directions.

THE PROS AND CONS OF BEING AN ANGER SNEAK

There are times when being sneaky with your anger makes a certain amount of sense. For instance, it might be better just to say, "Yes, yes, I'll do what you want" to an overbearing, controlling, interfering boss—and then just do what you would have done anyhow—than trying to explain your ideas to someone who you know won't listen. That tactic is particularly useful if your boss is also a bully who would punish or even fire you if you spoke up. (Needless to add, it would also be a good idea to print up one's resumé and start looking for a job with a better boss.) Sneaky anger, then, is best used in situations in which someone's efforts and honesty go unrewarded or get punished.

Sneaky anger is an option when someone else is more invested in your efforts and success than you are yourself. That's probably why teenagers often practice sneaky anger: "Yes, Mom, yes Dad, I promise I'll do that homework tonight. I know I've got to get good grades to get into college. (Now leave me alone so I can get back to instant messaging my friends. All I want to do is pass that stupid math class. Who cares about college anyhow? Just leave me alone before I lose control and tell you both where to shove that math book.)"

Some marriages feature one dominating partner (either male or female) and one anger sneak. The sneaky angry partner sometimes explains that forgetting, promising but not doing, or stalling are the best ways to resist his or her partner without facing that person's wrath. The sneaky angry partner says things like, "I just can't tell her no when she really insists I do something like mowing the lawn. She'd get too upset and then she'd never quit nagging me to do it. So I tell her I will mow that lawn this weekend. Maybe I will and maybe I won't." Sneaky anger lets this guy retain a sense of power and control over his world.

Sneaky anger is a bad way to handle anger, however, especially if it becomes a habit and a lifestyle. Here are a few of the costs that you pay when you become an anger sneak:

- *Continuing anger, frustration, and misery.* Anger sneaks often feel pretty unhappy inside. That's because their anger is never fully and directly expressed. It comes out sideways, if it comes out at all. This means anger sneaks almost never have conversations that begin: "I am angry with you because . . . and this is what I want . . ." With all that unfinished business inside them, they feel bitter, depressed, gloomy, and grumpy.

- *Loss of respect.* Anger sneaks are not held in high regard by others. In fact, they are often the target of contempt. "Oh, don't even bother to ask Shellie to do that report. You know she'll just piss and moan about it for weeks and then we'll have to do it anyhow. She's useless." Anger sneaks don't usually get very far in their lives or careers. They spend too much time grumpily avoiding doing things that other people, including their bosses, want them to do.

■ *Feeling weak and wimpy.* Anger sneaks seldom feel very powerful. Instead, they think that just about everyone else is stronger, more confident, and more determined than they are. Of course, this is bad for their self-esteem. Worse, because they feel weak and wimpy, they often fail in their efforts. The cabinet they were making goes uncompleted, the report remains half-finished. Each failure makes the anger sneak feel worse. Every failure leads to more failures.

■ *Isolation.* Anger sneaks are excellent distancers. They spend a lot of time hiding out in the basement, garage, or some corner of the house. Why? Because nobody can tell them what to do when they can't find them. But it gets pretty lonely after a while. Anger sneaks must come out of hiding so they can enjoy a better family and social life.

■ *Lack of positive energy.* Anger sneaks are pretty negative people. They spend a lot of time stubbornly refusing to do what others want them to do. The trouble with that is they don't spend enough time doing positive things. Sometimes they don't even know what they want, just what they don't want ("I don't want to mow the lawn but I don't know what else to do except watch TV").

Sneaky anger provides immediate benefits. It helps people not do, at least for a while, the things they don't want to do. However, sneaky anger is a very poor long-term way to deal with anger and conflict. People can develop a thoroughly negative lifestyle that is unsatisfying to themselves and everyone around them.

HOW TO QUIT BEING AN ANGER SNEAK

Anger sneaks can change by learning how to tell others directly what they want and feel. There are three main tasks for anger sneaks:

■ Break through denial of anger.

■ Challenge the sense of weakness.

■ Let go of the fun of frustrating others.

Breaking Through Denial of Anger

You must face facts. You are an angry person. True, your anger comes out sideways, but nevertheless you are angry. Every act of forgetting, every "I don't know," every time you play dumb are your ways of telling others you are mad.

You're probably angry about two things. First, people are always pushing you around. That pisses you off. But you're also angry at yourself. That's because you don't have the guts to tell them directly to mind their own business.

Acceptance of your anger comes first. You simply won't change until you honor the anger inside you. That anger is there for a purpose. It's trying to tell you to take control of your life. Anger sneaks who don't accept their anger are like road construction workers who only know how to dig holes. The more they work the deeper they go, but the road is going nowhere. You can learn to make a path with your anger, one that goes somewhere positive.

Challenging the Sense of Weakness

Sneaky anger is a weapon of the weak. Every time you use it you get weaker.

People become anger sneaks when they believe they cannot stand up to others. Maybe it starts with parents or older siblings who seem too big and strong to challenge. Then it's teachers and others in power. Then it's partners, colleagues at work, children, everybody.

Sneaky anger is always childlike. Anger sneaks don't take an adult position in life because they feel too small and inadequate.

So who are you scared of? Who can't you say no to? Why? What powers do they hold over you? When you're around them, how old do you feel?

It's time to take charge of your life. Too many years have been wasted saying "yeah, I'll do it later" when you wanted to say no. Too much time has been lost stalling, putting things off, not doing what others want but also not knowing what you want.

Gather your personal power, your courage, your determination. Becoming strong is the only way to give up sneaky anger. Learn to believe in yourself. True, others may object when you tell them exactly what you want. But it won't be any worse than what happens now. They're already angry with you because of your sneaky games and cons. Why not give them something real to confront, namely the truth.

Letting Go of the Fun of Frustrating Others

Now we get to a tough part. It's difficult to quit being an anger sneak because driving all those people nuts is enjoyable. Anger sneaks are trapped in their success. It feels good to defeat powerful opponents.

This anger style works. You've seen the little smile of the boy whose parents can't get him to clean his room. It's the same smile on the face of the woman who just can't balance the checkbook and the man who can't even get home on time. It's the smile that says, "I've got you. The more you want me to do something, the more I'll resist."

You win. You prove, again and again, that nobody can make you do anything you don't want to. How often, we wonder, do you have to keep proving this fact? And to whom?

You think you're winning, but every win is a loss. All you're doing is demonstrating your negativity. Maybe others can't make you do anything. But what do you want to do? What are your goals?

Here are just a few consequences of sneaky anger:

- Not knowing what you really want and need

- Not getting your wants and needs met because no one knows them

- Becoming critical, cynical, and negative about life

- Living with your own dishonesty, day after day

- Creating confusion for yourself as well as others

Take a few minutes to look at how you use your sneaky anger. Answer the questions below to find out about yourself.

1. How do I "blow people off" when I don't want to pay attention or do what they ask?

2. How do I "blow people off" while I'm pretending that I'm paying attention and that I will do what they want?

3. How do I avoid saying yes or no to other people?

4. What excuses do I make for my procrastination?

5. Which of the things I've identified in the first four questions am I willing to change even if someone wants me to change them?

Here is a chance to identify what you, personally, gain and lose when you use sneaky anger. First, check the things that you gain. Add any other gains you can think of to this list.

With my sneaky anger, I can

___	Avoid conflict right now	___	Stay a victim
___	Get my way	___	Get back at others
___	Avoid responsibility	___	Avoid decisions
___	Avoid mistakes	___	Stay in control

Now check the things that you lose when you use sneaky anger. Add any other losses to your list as well.

With my sneaky anger, I lose

___	Respect from others	___	Pride in myself
___	Respect for myself	___	Goodwill from others
___	Things I really do want	___	Good communication
___	Long-term gains	___	Praise from others
___	Opportunity to change	___	Good feelings for others

LET'S GET PRACTICAL

Yes, you can give up the sneaky anger style. But you'll have to practice new behavior. Here's the new game plan.

First, *say yes and no clearly when people ask something.* No exceptions. No excuses. That means you're willing and able to handle conflict directly. It also means saying no when you don't plan on doing something, not yes just to get them off your back for a while.

Get someone to have a yes/no fight with you. You start with yes and your partner with no. You say yes in as many ways as you can, while he or she says no, no, no-no-no. Absolutely no content allowed. You can't talk about anything specific. Just say yes and no, so you can get those words more firmly planted in your brain. Take a minute to discuss your reactions. Then switch sides. This time you say no while your partner says yes.

It takes courage to say yes and no directly, honestly, openly. But that's the bottom line. If you want to recover from sneaky anger you'll have to give up all those ways you've invented to camouflage anger. No more guerrilla tactics. No more sneak attacks. No more yes's that mean no's, maybe's that mean go to hell, later's that mean never.

Second, *tell people when you feel pushed around.* Sneaky anger usually occurs over issues of power and control. Anger sneaks feel that others are always telling them what to do. But usually they don't honestly confront others. Instead, they play games.

It's important to tell others to back off. After all, you have a right to make your own choices. Your life is your own.

Try this: Ask someone your size to push their hands firmly against yours. Have a shoving match. Practice pushing hard against that person. Use all the stubbornness inside you. Say out loud "you can't make me" and "I won't let you push me around anymore." Discover your power.

Third, *make your own choices.* You want all those people to leave you alone. You've just pushed them away. But there is much more to a good life than that. You need to decide what you want to do with yours. This third change is the hardest. That's because anger sneaks define themselves by what they don't do, not what they do. "You can't make me" all too often means "I exist." That's got to change, starting now. You need to find out who you are. Make decisions. Little ones. Big ones. Each choice helps you find out something more about what's important, who you are, what you want. You will begin to think of yourself as a choice-maker.

Here's a morning exercise for you. Divide a sheet of paper in two. Label one column "What they can't make me do today." That's to honor your need to be independent. The other side reads "What I choose to do today." That's to help you switch to being a person who does things on your own.

A long-term job for you is to set some new goals. What do you want to do? What do you want to get and give in relationships? What are your wishes, and how can you turn them into realities?

Here's the new game plan:

- Say yes and no clearly.

- Don't let people push you around.

- Make your own choices.

That's what it takes to quit being an anger sneak.

4

Anger Turned Inward

"When I'm really mad at others, I sometimes take it out on myself."

"I get just as mad at myself as I do at other people."

"I just hate my guts."

Anger turned inward means taking the feeling of anger, and behaving in a way that turns that anger on ourselves. The results are that we hurt ourselves, sometimes knowingly but often without thinking much about it. Although anger is a feeling, it can lead us to angry behaviors such as blaming, ignoring, shaming, criticizing, attacking, condemning, abandoning, and physically harming its target. What happens when we target ourselves for these kinds of punishments?

We often hear people say they are frustrated, angry, even furious with themselves. Some people get as angry with themselves as they do with others in their lives. But many say they are angry only with themselves. There are also those who refuse to admit any anger whatever, but treat themselves like yesterday's trash. They are angry and disgusted that they are here in this world, feeling inadequate and paralyzed, they try to justify the fact that they exist, and often feel like failures.

In this chapter we will talk about:

- When anger turned inward is useful/good anger.

- Why we turn our anger on ourselves inappropriately.

- How some people direct their anger inside without noticing.

- Why we are the easiest target for our own anger.

- How we harm ourselves with anger turned inward.

- The basics of taking better care of ourselves.

It is when we turn our anger inward often, with too much energy, calling ourselves names and feeling angry with ourselves for whatever we do, that our anger becomes a problem—for us and usually for those who love us, as well.

CAN ANGER TURNED INWARD BE HEALTHY?

Anger turned inward certainly can be healthy at a moderate level. If I've just yelled at my children for something that isn't their fault, then I have a good reason to be angry with myself. If I just spent the month's food money on one big party, I have reason to be angry at having made some bad choices. And if I have ignored somebody's really good advice for the umpteenth time and now I have lost something important just because I resent other people giving me any advice at all, being angry with myself may help me to learn something.

On the other hand, if I have just made a dumb mistake and have to do something over ... well, that happens to all of us sometime. I may feel frustrated and perhaps embarrassed that I did something wrong—but punishing myself won't help, and it isn't reasonable to call myself names or judge myself worthless.

Anger Is a Signal

Anger turned inward is like a light on your car's dashboard that starts flashing because a problem has occurred. Perhaps the engine temperature is rising too high on the gauge. Maybe there's no water in the radiator. If you don't check the problem out, how will you know whether your temperature is really too high or whether the indicator light is off-kilter? Maybe there's a wrong connection. Maybe *you* need cooling down. Or if the light never flashes so there is no signal at all, perhaps there is a short. We should all be able to become angry with ourselves when it helps to make us safer and better people. However, we don't want to be angry with ourselves all the time.

Anger turned inward and anger turned out toward others aren't really opposites. It's possible to have a lot of both. Most people who turn their anger on themselves, though, would rather hurt themselves than others. So the anger styles they most share with others tend to be anger avoidance, shame-based anger, and sneaky anger.

INAPPROPRIATE ANGER TURNED INWARD

When people take anger out on themselves, they may have trouble stopping.

"I am such a dummy. I never know what to say. Sometimes I'd like to slap myself. I should know better. When will I ever learn? I deserve this headache, that's for sure . . ."

Anger with themselves becomes a habit—just like any other habit. They get used to stuffing their anger, and calling themselves names. Soon that feels normal. It's easier than fighting with someone else, as well. Other people can talk back.

Here are some examples of people who turn their anger inward onto themselves:

Jamie doesn't want to upset anyone. Therefore, she continually says yes to things she doesn't want to do and to people she doesn't want to be around. She doesn't have any time to take responsibility for herself or even take good care of herself. If she isn't busy pleasing others, she's bailing them out of trouble. Sometimes Jamie would like to collapse . . . but she still continues working too hard and fails to take care of herself. She says she's not angry—that she doesn't get angry. But she also says she "doesn't matter," and treats herself as if that were true.

Karen says she'd never want to hurt herself, but she does do things wrong at times. When she feels that she has done things wrong, her mind gets confused, she thinks about too many things at once, and she has a lot of accidents. She'll burn herself cooking, scald her tongue, forget there's another step on the staircase and fall on the cement, she'll stab her other hand with a paring knife. Once she backed through her own garage door without realizing the door was down and smashed her new bike.

She just happens to hurt herself when she is angry about something and ignores it. These episodes can also happen when she has been angry with herself for letting other people "upset" her. Karen's actually pretty angry with them, but she also feels guilty or scared about her anger. Then she has an accident of some kind, and she feels less scared, and sometimes less guilty.

Wanda takes her anger out on herself by drinking, taking pills, and cutting herself. She knows she's mad, but doesn't want to hurt others more than she already has. She knows others already worry about her, but she doesn't want them to know what's going on inside her. So she releases her stressful feelings by attacking herself.

Jimmy thinks about how to kill himself instead of fighting with his parents. Yes, sometimes he thinks they'll deserve the pain if he does it, but when he lets his anger out, his mom just gets mad at him. His dad is sick and might get sicker or more upset, and he feels too guilty about that possibility. So, when he can't have his way, when he just knows his parents are unfair, he gets resentful and full of rage. He feels worthless, unlovable, and like he just shouldn't be. When he feels that way, he just sits and thinks about different ways to die. Since this is anger directed at himself, he doesn't have to feel so guilty.

Amy uses her credit card instead of doing what she'd really like to with her life—she pays and pays for her belief that she's worthless and can't fit in anywhere.

Thomas sabotages himself whenever things begin to really go right. He blames the rest of the world for the things that go wrong. However, if he looked carefully, he could see that he is setting himself up and taking out his anger on himself.

There are many patterns of behavior that contribute to turning anger inward on yourself. Here's a quiz to help you see whether you have some behavior patterns that contribute to turning your anger on yourself.

Anger Turned Inward Quiz

☐ I don't like to hurt anybody's feelings.

☐ Other people might get mad, but I don't.

☐ It's hard for me to really care about myself.

☐ Sometimes I might act a little unhappy if I feel angry.

☐ I tell myself I shouldn't get angry even if somebody else would.

☐ When I say somebody makes me sick, I mean it literally. I just can't let go of the stress.

☐ All I really want is peace with no conflict.

☐ Even when I'm angry with someone, I feel like I should make sure they are doing okay.

☐ I get mad at myself for things I would comfort others about.

☐ Other people don't know I wear a mask, because I am so good at it.

☐ Usually I just keep all my feelings to myself.

☐ I feel guilty when I feel angry or resentful.

☐ I am ashamed of myself when I get angry. I should be better than that.

☐ I'm too busy to take care of myself, even if I know I should.

☐ I'm always doing things wrong.

☐ I have an addictive behavior I use when I'm angry. It makes me feel better at the moment, but later I feel worse.

☐ I tend to have accidents when I get angry, like hammering my finger.

☐ Some days I get so angry that I would like to hurt myself.

☐ If I hurt myself, maybe other people won't hurt me.

☐ It's hard for me to care about myself.

☐ I don't care what I do, just so long as I don't hurt anybody else.

Put a checkmark next to the statements that apply to you. Count them. If you have three or more items checked, look at how you can change to treat yourself better. If you have six or more checkmarks, it's likely that you have some anger-turned-inward habits that affect your life negatively. If you have eight or more checkmarks, you definitely have some anger-turned-inward habits to change. Changing a few things could make you feel a lot better about your life.

YOU MAY SAY TO YOURSELF, "SO I'M TURNING MY ANGER ON MYSELF? WHY?"

Most of us hide our anger from ourselves because we don't want to look at ourselves. For example, if Don sees he's really angry with his friend Tim for giving so many orders and he says he doesn't like that to Tim, Don might rock the boat. If Tim got upset with Don for speaking up, who would Don have to hang around with then? Maybe Don also thinks he has no right to get angry with someone else. Back when he was a kid, he learned that if anything goes wrong, he'll be to blame. No matter what goes wrong, it'll be his fault. So why would he want to bring up something Tim will just get mad about. Better to keep it in, even if he does get a headache.

Some of us are like Sherry, who thinks that being angry with anyone else equals being mean and hurting them. She's been hurt by angry people herself. Forget it. She just won't do that to anyone else. Inside, though, she sits in judgment of herself—and nothing is right! So she yells at herself a lot and doesn't eat and exercises way too much. She is just furious she can't make herself perfect.

Maybe people who are angry with themselves have learned from a relative that getting angry at others means "losing control," or that "only dogs get mad." They may even have seen people who were openly angry described as "crazy" and "irrational."

We believe that people who turn their anger on themselves have often been taught that being angry with someone else is morally bad. Many have learned that to protest what seems unfair by "talking back" is just "looking for trouble." And if they go looking for trouble, they fear they'll find plenty of punishment. Not wanting others to be angry with them, or to punish them, sometimes they punish themselves, just to show that no one else has to.

In addition, moral self-righteousness, self-attack, rage and abuse, and vulnerability have played their part in many people's lives so that they learn one or more of the following beliefs:

1. I am a morally better person if I turn my anger on myself rather than becoming angry with others.

2. We often have been taught as children that we have no right to protest things that others do and say. We have been told that this is rude, ungrateful, wrong, disloyal, insulting, or irrational. So we learned to either suppress our anger or to attack ourselves for any feelings of anger we have. We have learned not to be inappropriate, and we try to avoid being punished by others.

3. We might have learned that when we object or disagree with something, we will be called names, hit, slapped, or that love will be withdrawn from us. It is safer to be angry with ourselves. We would rather target ourselves than be targets for others.

4. We've learned that expressing anger may change the relationship with another person. We don't want to disrupt the relationship because then we don't know what will happen. We feel vulnerable. We worry what the result will be. Rather than risk changing anything in the relationship, we have decided just to turn the anger on ourselves, or stuff it.

5. Like children, we may think that if we have done something wrong and we punish ourselves, then the world (or parent) won't punish us as much. If we punish ourselves, we have the sense that we are more in control of what happens.

6. We often feel shameful and unacceptable. Because we do, we turn our anger against ourselves in self-hatred, in the belief that we must somehow justify our continued existence. We feel defective, and we are angry at ourselves for being that way.

This is a painful list of reasons for becoming angry with ourselves and hurting ourselves. But notice that a lot of things on this list are things we can choose not to believe and have not believed or acted on consciously because we were hurt by others. At times, we even feel too responsible to hurt anyone because we have gone through these feelings. It's no wonder that we are angry. Perhaps we are not so much at fault after all. Maybe what we've learned to think and believe is what's wrong.

We will discuss the ways we can change shortly. First, let's take a look and see what others see from the outside, when we are very angry with ourselves.

DEPRESSION AND ANXIETY CAN CAUSE US TO TURN OUR ANGER AGAINST OURSELVES

Depression can make you feel as though you can't do anything right. It creates feelings of anger in some people, too. If you have a clinical depression, you are more likely to have suicidal thinking, and to harm yourself by cutting, biting, scratching, and hitting. You also are more likely to use drinking and drugging (including prescriptions) too much in an attempt to change those feelings.

Anxiety can create panic, inability to be in social environments, overwhelming fear, and agitation. This can lead to similar problems related to self-medication and addiction. Some people who are too anxious to handle emotional pain may cut themselves to "release the pain, " or to make it physical pain instead of just emotional. This, in a way, makes the pain "real." It can be an indication someone needs help, or a vengeful action wrapped up in self-attack.

Too often as a part of risk taking, belonging, and needing attention (mostly from peers), school kids may even play games where they get intense with each other about cutting, vomiting, burning themselves, and other kinds of self-punishment. This is really anger turned inward by those who haven't figured out what to do with their strong feelings yet. Along with a desire for peer and/or parent attention and wanting to belong, we have seen situations in which many kids in a group try these methods to handle their feelings. Many of these kids are depressed or have really low self-esteem.

If hurting yourself in ways like these sounds like you, see a counselor, a pastor, a parent, or a healthy friend to talk to; someone else who has recovered from the same kinds of things. Find time to talk to people who can tell you about how to stop your bad habits and will help you develop better ways to take care of yourself. Reading this book may help you realize how you are harming yourself, but you need wise and caring people in person to help stop these actions and to manage life better.

What are the patterns that harm us when we turn our anger on ourselves? Why isn't turning anger inward any better than one of the other anger styles? The simple answer is that when we don't recognize our anger, and don't use it properly, we hurt ourselves. Anger is a helpful guide to reasoned behavior. But when we misuse it, we can hurt ourselves, and often when we hurt ourselves, we hurt our families, too.

There are five primary patterns we use when we turn our anger on ourselves. They are:

- Self-neglect

- Self-sabotage

- Self-blame

- Self-attack

- Self-destruction

Self-neglect

Remember how people try to ignore others (especially kids) rather than get really angry with them? That is how self-neglect starts. First, you begin to ignore yourself. Why pay attention? Your mind is making noise, your body is yelling, your spirits are sinking. But you're not so important as the things you have to do.

You start paying more attention to others than to yourself. Life at first seems easier if you don't know how you feel. If what you want takes the back seat, maybe everybody else will be happy. If there's no conflict, you don't have to notice that you're angry. You get better at getting things done, and work even harder. It becomes easy to do this, because what you are working on (family, work, career, home care, schooling, kid's education and recreation, etc.) is more important than you. It gets easier to believe that. Soon you're working as hard as you can, and there's conflict anyway. Nobody is ever satisfied, it seems. You sleep less. You sleep less well. You eat poorly or in a hurry because you are less important. You don't have the time to exercise anymore. Some days you don't really care where your life is going—you just want to get through the day. And *oops*, you were late to your doctor's appointment again. Maybe you shouldn't even make those appointments. Going to the doctor gets expensive. And it takes time you think you don't have.

Meantime, you are busy, and no matter whether you have many or few responsibilities you struggle with, they begin to seem overwhelming. But you would feel guilty letting go of something. What could you let go of? Or you believe that you can't let go and still pay the bills. You get anxious and depressed; maybe you get a cold, and it won't go away. Others start worrying about you. They ask how you are, and that's embarrassing. You smile and say "fine." You don't want to impose on them for help. You are supposed to be able to handle this yourself. And often, you don't identify feeling angry at all. You just feel overwhelmed. But you don't stop and take care of yourself. You don't clear your calendar. You won't do less than the perfect thing. You know that you are only human, but you persist in treating yourself like a machine.

This self-neglect is an angry way to treat yourself. Your basic wants and needs aren't taken care of, and you don't care about how you make yourself feel. You might have some resentment, or feel bitter about your responsibilities, but who keeps you where you are? Sometimes the truth is, you've trained everyone else to depend on you. You haven't paid attention to their worry about you. And you are about to get what? Bronchitis? Pneumonia? Another part-time job? You will not be able to be a very good caretaker because you have neglected yourself too much.

This first pattern of self-neglect is very hard to change, and it is very important to change it. That means you must find a way to consider yourself important, besides doing for others.

Here's what needs to be done:

- Notice how you have been giving yourself the cold shoulder, and ignoring your own needs. Ask yourself how you came to believe that you should treat yourself less well than others. If the answer is that doing this is more socially or morally correct, keep digging until you figure out where your shame is coming from.

- Slow down enough so that you can start to recognize how you are feeling and begin to eat when you need to, and sit for a minute when you need to.

- Start doing positive things to care for yourself. Realize that for a little while you will have a feeling of guilt when you say no to something, and you must say that no anyway. When you do, don't rush to help someone else. Take time for a slower meal, a nap, a bath, a walk around the block, a talk with someone you miss, or your favorite TV show—the one that makes you laugh.

■   Understand that you need to treat both yourself and others just as you treat anything valuable—with gentleness, caring, and love. If at bedtime you have not done one good thing for yourself today that you can count, you're backsliding. Start again tomorrow morning. We know this is really hard for self-neglecters. One last good note is that we know an older lady who, after years of hard work and community and church involvement, cleared up her schedule by learning to say no enough to give herself a little room to live. She has always been able to paint—she was born with this talent— but she tells us that after years of frustration and responsibility, she has now, for the first time, learned what it is to experience "joy." She is regularly painting for herself as well as for churches, schools, hospitals, and nursing homes. At eighty-two, she feels that she is starting life all over and she says that "it's the first time I really ever had fun!"

Self-sabotage

Self-sabotage is a way of using sneaky anger on yourself. For example, Skye is a bundle of energy. She wants to do everything and do it well. The problem is, the more she wants to personally accomplish a particular project, the less likely it is that she will really finish it. As wonderfully talented as she is, she can't seem to complete many projects. Either she didn't start until it was really too late to do a good job (painting her house in Wisconsin in late October) or she leaves out something vital (filling out a renewal form for her professional work, and losing it just before the deadline for mailing).

More and more, she sees what she is doing as a failed attempt from the start. She used to say, "Sure, I'll do it!" but now she says, "Well, I'll try." She is often embarrassed when things don't go right, but still tries to make big changes at the last minute. Anything that is almost finished is in danger of falling apart, going missing, getting lost, or being finished sloppily. She can't see the good parts of what she does much anymore. She looks at every mistake. Her self-esteem just goes down and down.

She can "dream" of what she really wants to do someday, but it's harder and harder to get started. Her friends and family know that when she gets all excited about something, it probably won't really happen. If they help, she will feel worse about herself. Now she both loves and hates finding a new project, because she never seems to truly get anywhere. This feeling of frustration and loss is very familiar.

Tony, her neighbor, has trouble doing much of anything. It's not that he doesn't want to get anywhere. He knows that he will write a really great novel, and that if he could just save enough cash for an initial investment, he could be very successful in the bakery business. The equipment is costly, though. And the closest he really has gotten to opening a bakery is delivering bread and snacks to convenience stores.

He thought he'd be further along by now, but he's forty-two, and still just making it. He knows he never accomplishes his dreamy fantasies and occasionally wonders if there's something wrong with him. He is going to therapy. So he'll just go to have another "deep" talk, and then he'll have a drink instead of thinking about that stuff. Tomorrow is another day. Maybe it will be better. But it isn't.

Tony keeps getting into relationships with women who have problems. They are angry all the time. Two of them were chronic alcoholics, and all three were blamers. Tony himself doesn't believe in being angry, so he just sucks it up. He has tried to "fight fair" and tries to teach his partners fair fighting. He tries to calm their fears, and to meet their expectations (impossible). He actually does show active caring. He wants to be the guy who teaches them men aren't all bad. Still, he is accused of being neglectful, being abusive, using women, being lazy, not caring. Although Tony is not perfect, and does admit to having used women in the past, he also truly does choose angry blamers. It took him seven years to leave the last of these partners, because he really did not want to hurt her feelings, and he was hoping she would begin to realize that some men are different. He endures all this because he can indisputably tell himself that he is a good person. It is the others who misunderstand him. He hates living this way. But what else can he do to make him feel worthwhile when he's such a failure?

Both Skye and Tony prevent themselves from really getting anywhere. Skye does it for herself, and Tony finds a partner who will undermine him regularly, just in case he doesn't do a good enough job of self-sabotage himself. Both of them know that something's wrong. Neither has seemed able to change right away.

The pattern of self-sabotage is often not understood very well. That is because shame, anger, rebellion, resentment, and paralysis are all part of it, whether a person acts energetic or forgetful. First, many self-saboteurs have been told over and over that they inevitably do things wrong, and how they must do things to do them right. They feel shame over having not done things right, or having been considered inadequate by somebody else.

They have become oversensitive to the idea that a comment is both a command and an expectation that they must meet. The sense of being ordered to do things is also shaming, and resentment and self-berating anger are not far behind. But this anger is hidden in a mask of trying and failing, of sincere effort and inadequacy. Initially, this mask was worn to hide the shame, hurt, and anger of someone who was not allowed to express these feelings. Somewhere along the way, though, they turned the commanding voice into their own voice inside themselves. Self-sabotage is one way to say "You can't make me," even though the saboteur is saying that to himself as well as to other people.

Two other strategies support the person's inability to deliver: confusion and paralysis. The confusion comes into play when distraction is used in order to soften the shame of not achieving the goal (even if the person wants to meet the goal). Paralysis comes from the anxiety inherent in the situation where a person must both *do* something and *not do* something to fulfill their mental script.

If you're good at self-sabotage, you probably feel much worse about yourself than you would if you were able to learn to say a real yes and a real no and a real "let me be for now" to others. In fact, that's hard, because self-sabotage occurs because a person doesn't want to do something and also doesn't want to have conflict.

■ It's important to remember that you are a grown-up, and to do your project without letting the fears of a child get in the way. Indeed, if this project is yours, you may do it or not do it. You may do it the way you want to. You no longer have to "forget" to be free, or have to be yelled at or shamed because you do it your way. If a particular project is not yours, say no to taking it on right now. Don't set yourself up as a hero and become a martyr. And don't blame the other guy if you have said yes or refused to say no and stick to it.

- Let your grown-up organize the project. Let the kid inside you help a little, and not be perfect. Keep everything together in one small area, and when you want to quit, take a break and start again. Even if you think you don't want to do your project, you will probably enjoy it when you get into it again. Get used to more success than usual by finishing it.

- Learn to say to yourself, "every day in every way I deserve success." Say it until you believe it. If that doesn't work, start with "Life is not my fault." Sing the word "no" to a song with a rhythm that you like. We like "deck the halls with boughs of holly, no no no no no, no no, no no." This is good practice for real decisions. You can bet that saying what you really feel becomes easier as you and others get used to it.

- When you get scared or paralyzed, remember that to undo paralysis, you gotta exercise. If it's a blank sheet of paper, or someone new you have to talk to over the phone, go for it— and once you begin don't stop till you finish that particular thing. It can be revised later. Brainstorm the event, don't criticize.

- Most important, remind yourself that the bad feelings and the self-pity that come with self-sabotage are not rewards, and think of some rewards to give yourself that are better.

Self-blame

The third habit pattern in turning anger inward is self-blame. This is really very simple. People who have this pattern of behavior simply believe that if anything goes wrong, they are guilty. Check the expressions below to see whether these are familiar to you, and if you say them to yourselves.

- ☐ If I weren't here, everything would be better.

- ☐ If I had been there when it happened, nothing bad would have happened.

- ☐ If I weren't such a dummy . . .

- ☐ I know better than that.

- ☐ How could anybody love me?

- ☐ I'm an idiot.

- ☐ I'm just being stupid.

- ☐ I can't do anything right.

- ☐ I deserve to be (punished, left, yelled at, abandoned, etc.).

- ☐ How could I do that?

- ☐ What's wrong with me, anyway?

- ☐ See what I've done now?

- ☐ I said/did it wrong again.

- ☐ I could just curl up and die.

- ☐ Swearing (saying nasty words to yourself, calling yourself names).

Most people who self-blame also take way too much responsibility for others. Somehow, they have learned that if anything is wrong, it is their fault, and that it is up to them to make sure that things go well and no one is unhappy. This gets pretty technical. If something in the food is wrong, you should have caught that before it got to the table, even though this isn't your kitchen. Your buddy wouldn't have slipped and cut his knee if you had been there to help him, and why weren't you? If two other people are starting to have an argument and you can't distract them well enough to stop the arguing, you shouldn't even have been there.

Change means changing some very basic thinking patterns, and each one will have to be tested and retested until you are comfortable about the change.

- ■ Ask yourself, "Who told me I was responsible for that?" "Who told me that?"

- ■ Ask, "Do I really still believe that?" "Do I think that way about other people?" "Would I blame them?" "My friend Andrea isn't guilty for that, why am I?" "How could I have known what would occur?"

Then help yourself out:

- ■ Tell yourself it's not your fault. Tell yourself you are here to learn something and to give something, not to feel guilty for everything.

- Tell yourself you deserve a medal for surviving all the guilt and shame.

- Imagine giving yourself a hug. Then, give yourself a hug.

- Tell yourself, "I can only do what I can do."

  - "I'm good enough for me today."

  - "I am perfectly human."

  - "I'm not guilty, and I'm able to respond."

- Remember that someone taught you how to scold yourself this way. Who was it? Why were you afraid? Do you really have to be afraid of that person now?

- Think of your internal "scolder" as a guard dog who makes you behave so other people won't get mad and scold you. Think about how you would like to retrain your guard dog, and what would be a really helpful thing it could watch out for? What are reasonable rules for its job?

Self-attack

Self-attack is the fourth habit pattern formed when anger is turned inward. While this pattern can be formed as an adult, it is more likely that it was formed when the person was much younger. A lot of those who engage in self-attack learned to do this through experiences of being harshly abused, perhaps in many ways.

Self-attack occurs when people attack themselves both physically and verbally. Self-attack can include many physical kinds of attack. For example, burning yourself "accidentally" if you are upset with yourself; banging your head or your fist on a wall and injuring yourself. One person was so upset with herself for getting angry at her children that she threw herself out the car door. Putting a lit cigarette out on your own chest is self-attack.

The basic idea behind self-attack is that one's self must be punished and deserves to be attacked. The feeling is no longer anger— the individual is enraged with the self. Things said to the self are those that will hurt the most. Injuries to the self are common, because blood is often a part of self-attack. Hurting oneself becomes a way to demonstrate how bad one is to others.

Again, there may be the factor that "if I hurt myself, you will not hurt me." Also, for some people, using self-attack may be the only way of hanging on to and keeping the emotional legacy of an abusive parent.

Some self-attackers may not be able to avoid partners who will hurt them. However, this is not an excuse for the partner who then steps in and does hurt them. There is no excuse for being violent with your partner. In this case, the abusive partner has found someone to dominate and to harm, and the self-attacker may not have experienced relationships without attack, or may not know how to have a relationship where they are not attacked by others.

Also, an attack by another person seldom completely resolves the problem of someone who has learned to self-attack. Self-attack can occur at differing levels, for example:

■ Scratching oneself to wounds is sometimes an alternative to cutting, one ordinarily less lethal and less precise than cutting, but perhaps just as bloody.

■ Putting oneself in very risky situations again and again may be a part of self-attack. The person who self-attacks demonstrates self-punishment and expects the same.

How this works inside a person differs. Some people may self-attack wanting more than anything that some other person will step in and, for the first time, help to stop their suffering. Another person may self-attack by throwing himself through a plate glass window because he really wishes he could blot out an enemy. Other people may have internalized angry and sometimes sadistic family members, gang members, partners, or friends. Having believed what those other persons said, now they treat themselves as if they were the punisher. The original punisher also may have made the self-attacker do things that were cruel or lethal to another person or animal, and the hate for having done that "task" propels the self-attack now.

What is most important here is to get help for the self-attacker. That person needs help to do the following:

■ Figure out what the punisher inside is like, so he or she can begin to understand and reject that punisher.

■ Decrease how often and how intense their attacks on themselves are.

- Notice what conditions make self-attack more likely: for example, a telephone call, drinking, or smelling something in particular can act as a trigger. What triggers the self-attacking is very important, since that is a key to undoing the problem.

- Learn how to choose friends who are not punishing and not critical. Self-attackers can thrive when there is someone who can see and appreciate how good they are, and who will not help in self-punishment at all.

Self-destruction

Anger turned inward in self-destruction is very harsh. Usually those who participate in self-destruction have extreme shame as well as anger, and consider themselves all bad, and others all good. Therefore, others cannot understand them, and because they are all bad, they refuse to take in any caring, love, praise, or comfort from the people around them.

This causes great hopelessness and despair, and we think that hopelessness is the most lethal of all emotions. People feel as if they "should not be," and lose hope that life will ever get any better. As a result, they cannot see anything good, and also are not able to think very well. An attempt at self-destruction can result in serious physical and/or mental disability. Don't think you are immune to that.

We have seen a very smart person become mentally retarded. Actually, it is too hard to tell you what we have seen in this area. It is important to remember, though, that the emotion of hopelessness is lethal and when you realize you feel that way, right then is the time to find something to do to change the hopelessness to love, gratitude, courage . . . even anger, so long as you don't turn it inward. Realization is a moment of strength, a time for some new action, or a return to people who would comfort you if only you would let them in.

The answer to "I should not be" is "I am." But this is not an easy change, and to get there one has to learn to look simply at the self—to look at yourself without judgment, without approval, without disapproval. Just to be is okay. As long as you exist, you are. Make bigger sentences later.

Dialectic behavior therapy is often helpful, along with other therapies that stress nonjudgment. It helps to learn that you must take in caring, and acknowledge that you affect others and other's lives. It also helps to know that it is because the world is split in two that it feels as if you are all bad, and that you can learn a different kind of thinking.

The self-destructive person needs to give a voice to the despair, and to have help to challenge that despair. There is almost always an inner self that wants to preserve life. The person in this category needs to be assessed for depression, and will need the help of others. Asking for that help is a way of growing.

III

Explosive Anger Styles

5

Sudden Anger

Explosive anger styles are very different from masked ones. Exploders know they are mad and they tell others about it. They easily become enraged. Exploders shout and yell, swear, throw things, break objects, threaten, shove, pinch, bite, and hit.

We describe four explosive anger styles in this section. This chapter is about people with sudden anger. This kind of anger comes on quickly and goes away fast. Like the magician on stage, people with sudden anger perform a "now you see it, now you don't" trick.

Shame-based anger is the topic of chapter 6. Overly sensitive people may explode in rage when they feel criticized, put down, or ignored. Their anger comes from *not* feeling good enough about themselves.

Chapter 7 covers deliberate anger. People with this anger style get angry on purpose. "I want what I want and I want it now. Give it to me or else I'll explode" is what they are saying with their anger.

Excitatory anger, described in chapter 8, is the fourth explosive anger style. These people seek the anger "rush." They want that surge of adrenaline that comes when they explode with rage.

Explosive anger styles have value. For instance, sudden anger has immediate survival value. Scientists point out that people's brains begin responding to danger signals within less than one second after danger is perceived. That allows almost instantaneous physical reactions, an excellent idea if, for example, the drunk at the next barstool is coming at you with a broken beer bottle. That's a great time for your aggressive instincts to kick in so you can protect yourself. Getting angry on some occasions, then, may even save your life. At least exploders let the world know their feelings. But explosions are dangerous. People get hurt. Relationships get wrecked. Jobs are lost. If you're an exploder, read these chapters carefully. You may want to make a few changes.

I JUST LOST CONTROL—AGAIN

Theresa's got a problem. She blows up like a firecracker, but not just on the Fourth of July. She blows up any time of the day or night, almost every day.

Here's what she says: "I'm in trouble. I lose my head just about every time I get frustrated. One minute I'm talking normally. Everything's okay. I feel fine. The next I'm screaming my head off at Joe or the kids. It's better at work, but last week I told my boss she was the sorriest excuse for a supervisor I've ever seen. She sent me home for the day."

When Theresa gets angry she feels out of control, as if she's being swept out to sea by a powerful undertow. "My God," she thinks, "what am I doing? Why do I say such terrible things? Am I losing my mind?" But she can't stop. Unplanned, unexpected, the anger seems to take over. And then it's gone. Poof! The anger disappears.

"Whew," Theresa says to herself, "I'm glad that's over." Sometimes she feels better, relieved. She's gotten rid of her frustrations, tensions, anxieties. More often, though, she looks around and sees the hurt looks on people's faces. Then she feels awful.

But here's what amazes Theresa. Some of those people she yelled at are still upset. They actually want to talk about what happened. Why? Theresa's not angry anymore. It's over. What's the big deal? Her anger's gone. What good would it do to talk?

The goals of this chapter are to understand sudden anger and to offer suggestions to gain better control of anger. To do this, we'll need to solve two puzzles:

- Why do some people have more trouble controlling angry outbursts than others?

- Why do people with sudden anger blow up so unpredictably?

Let's begin with the first puzzle.

I Didn't Know the Gun Was Loaded

You're walking down the street, minding your own business. Boom! A bolt of anger smacks you right on the head. It makes you go crazy. You rant and rave. You can't help it. It hits so hard you explode. That's what people with sudden anger say it feels like.

Frankly, when we began treating angry people this sounded phony to us. How could anyone not see their anger coming? After all, there are plenty of warning signs that you're getting angry: physical changes, such as breathing fast and rising voice tone; emotional cues, such as feeling panicky or getting a headache; angry thoughts, like "I don't have to take this stuff anymore." All of these changes tell people they're getting mad. It was hard to believe anyone could ignore them. It sure sounded like a desperate attempt to avoid taking responsibility. "Don't blame me. I can't help it. I just get angry so fast I can't stop."

Later, though, we changed our minds. There are simply too many Theresas in this world, too many people who swear their anger catches them by surprise over and over again. We had to believe them.

A tremendous amount of research on the human brain has been conducted over the last decade. It is evident from this research that some people's brains are simply not as good as others at controlling anger and aggression. For instance, some people have relatively weak activity in a place near the front of the brain (the prefrontal cortex) that helps us to control our impulses. Others have overactive parts of the emotional center of the brain (the limbic system) so that their emotions are felt extremely quickly and intensely. There are several other problems in the brain that could make someone more prone to sudden anger attacks. Medications can help people who have some of these difficulties.

You might need to consult a physician to consider an appropriate medication trial if you have been trying for a long time to quit getting so strongly angry but have not been able to control your temper. However, for the remainder of this chapter we will assume that you can learn to slow down your angry reactions with commitment and education.

Let's make one simple assumption for the rest of this chapter: Nobody gets mad by accident. Anger never just happens. It doesn't come out of nowhere. There are always warning signs, but you have to look for them. And that's the problem.

People with sudden anger don't see any warning signs because they don't look for them.

We've often watched the anger build up in people with sudden anger. They're really no different than anyone else. They make fists. They pace the floor. They worry and fret and mutter to themselves. Their eyebrows furrow. Their eyes narrow and glare. But there is a difference. Unlike others, they don't notice these signs. They don't realize their inner tension is rising.

Those with sudden anger don't know the gun is loaded. They don't realize the gun has a hair trigger. Worst of all, they don't even know they're carrying a gun.

The answer to the puzzle, why do some people have more trouble controlling their anger than others, is that they don't pay attention to the warning signs.

We'll suggest ways to notice anger's warning signs later in this chapter, but there is more to understand about sudden anger first.

Solving the second puzzle, why do people with sudden anger blow up so unpredictably, begins with looking at the nature of frustration and violent impulses.

Frustration and Violent Impulses

Impulse: something done on the spur of the moment.

Violent impulse: a sudden and unreasoning desire to hurt someone.

You're quietly sitting on the sofa, listening to boring Aunt Matilda telling that old story about the time four ladies brought lemon

Jell-O salad to the picnic. Suddenly you feel a strong desire to scream, or kick dear Aunt Matilda, or run out of the room, or all three. That's a violent impulse.

Almost everybody has angry and violent impulses. Even Aunt Matilda, who may have secretly desired to throttle you a few times. But she didn't, and you didn't, because you live by the rules. The rules say you must control your impulses. You can think what you want, but you can't say or do mean things.

It's easy to see what happens when the rules fail. Just pick up the paper and read about the teenager who killed another teenager after a thirty-second argument. Society as we know it would be impossible if we all lived that way.

Probably everyone gives in to an angry impulse once in a while. Dad snaps at the kids when they ask for their allowance as soon as he gets home. Althea swats her boyfriend on the shoulder because his snoring wakes her up. Fifteen-year-old Cynthia swears at her kid sister for stealing her favorite sweater.

Teens often have trouble with sudden anger as hormonal changes kick in. Children have even more trouble controlling their impulses. They try to stop but sometimes the urge to attack wins. Then they strike out at whatever frustrates them.

Infants can't control their impulses at all. If they get hungry, they cry. If that doesn't get immediate results, they rage. And once they begin they can't stop. Mom or Dad shows up with a bottle, but they're too riled to drink. First they must be held and soothed. They still complain even after they start drinking. But then suddenly it's over, as if nothing bad happened.

People with the sudden anger style have adult impulse controls, but sometimes they seem to forget about them. Moments of frustration bring out the little kid in them. Ernie, the bus driver, is a good example. He throws his tools around whenever he can't quickly fix his car. Tim, the golfer, is a nice guy except when he's on the course. Miss a putt and he breaks his club in two.

"I can't stand frustration. I want everything to be all right, now!" That's how people with sudden anger get. They can't handle frustration. If they have to wait too long, or if they don't get what they want, they blow. Not all the time, though. If they tried that they'd be behind bars for a long while. Those with a sudden anger style don't lose control every time they get frustrated. It's more like playing dice. Once in a while they crap out. And when they do, watch out!

If you're like this, you know how unpredictable your blowups can be. Sure, some frustrations regularly set you off, like your oldest son sneaking out of the house again. Or being turned down for sex. But you handle other frustrations pretty well most of the time. You don't get bent out of shape every time your daughter forgets to fold the laundry or your buddy in the car pool comes late. But once in a while you do, and that's when the skyrockets explode. You feel thwarted. Your needs aren't being met.

Why did you blow this time and not last? One possible answer is chance. It just happened this time. But that's not very helpful. There's not much you can do to control your explosions if they are mostly a matter of bad luck.

It's not really luck, though. Remember that people with sudden anger have been ignoring the signs that their anger is building up. They are frustrated, yes, but not only about the nail that won't go in straight or their spouse getting home late. They're also mad about the dog who barked this morning, and the cold soup at lunch, and the boss who wants three things done at the same time, and the slow crawl home on overcrowded streets. Too much stress. Too many headaches. And then they explode. No wonder their anger seems way out of line. They're taking out their whole day's frustrations in a one- or two-minute blast.

Impatience

People with sudden anger are generally impatient. They don't handle frustration very well. They're quick to blow up at themselves and others. Here's an example.

Beth's a single mother with three kids. She works long and hard hours at a poorly paid job. She hears demands all day from customers. Sometimes she'd like to shout at them, but she keeps on smiling. The one thing she wants is to come home to a clean house. But tonight she walks in on a pillow fight in the living room. What a mess.

"Alexander, pick that chair up *now*," Beth yells. "Rachel, take those pillows to your room."

"Aw, Ma, we're just having fun," they say. "Quit being such a grump." Then Rachel throws a pillow at her head.

"That's it. I said now and I mean now. You're both grounded for the night. You stupid kids. You know I work hard. All I want is a little peace and quiet. Why, you never think of me. You're just selfish little brats."

Beth raves on for the next five minutes. Then she throws herself on her bed and cries. And then it's over, except that Alexander and Rachel avoid her the rest of the night.

Beth is impatient, like most people with sudden anger. She wants things *now*. No dawdling allowed. She feels personally insulted when people are slow doing what she expects.

To be fair, Beth's pretty impatient with herself, too. She doesn't like things that take a long time to do. That's one reason she dropped out of school. And she throws down her sewing in utter frustration when she makes a mistake. She's often fidgety, nervous, and restless. She also does things without thinking, on impulse. Once she quit her job, just like that, because of something her boss said. She called up the next day and got her job back, but she got a warning to watch her temper.

Impatience. Frustration. Violent impulses. Ignoring signs that anger is building. These are the Four Horsemen of sudden anger.

EASY COME, EASY GO? DON'T BET ON IT

Renee: I don't understand you, Harry. First you blow up over nothing. You go ballistic over little stuff. And then it's over, like it never happened. How can you get so mad and then act like it was nothing?

Harry: It's like this bomb explodes inside me. I feel a lot more relaxed after it goes off. I've said what I wanted to say. It's over. I'm just not mad anymore.

Ventilating. Letting off steam. It's one of the oldest ideas we have about anger. It's supposed to be healthy to let your anger out. You'll get sick if you hold it in. Just let your anger out, whenever you need to.

Ventilating is strictly an emotional event. Exploders are not solving problems with their anger. They don't first explode and then settle down to discuss their problems. They just want to release the tension that's been building up in their brains and bodies.

That's why sudden anger goes away so fast. It gets rid of a bad feeling. Ventilating sounds good. Why not let off a little steam now and then? But it can be a big mistake. Ventilating creates three major problems.

The first problem is that exploders often feel worse, not better. True, they're not angry anymore. But they feel guilty, stupid, out of control, childlike, irresponsible. Having a tantrum isn't exactly adult behavior. Here is an example. Doris gets mad at her kids when she is frustrated. They never know just when it will happen, but it happens repeatedly. Afterwards she feels terrible. She apologizes. She says she's wrong and she doesn't mean to blow up. Later, when her kids have a fight with each other, Doris blows up again. And she tells them, "An apology isn't enough." She never notices how she is teaching them to have tantrums. But somehow, she always feels guilty when they fight so much "about nothing."

The second problem with ventilating is even worse. People with sudden anger use their rages for only one reason: to let off steam. They don't value anger as a messenger telling them that something is wrong and needs work. Getting angry is their solution to problems. But anger's not meant to solve problems. Anger is a great signal but a lousy solution. Exploders create many more problems than they solve by blowing up.

There's one more big problem with sudden anger. Every time you ventilate your anger you're just teaching yourself to be more angry. Carol Tavris, author of *Anger: The Misunderstood Emotion*, says that ventilating anger "rehearses" it. The more you practice sudden explosions, the more times you will explode. It's not true that ventilating anger makes you less angry. It helps you release your anger for a few minutes. But every time you explode you're training yourself to be more explosive. The madder you are, the madder you get.

People with a sudden anger style explode to feel better. But they usually end up feeling worse, making more problems, training themselves to get angry all the time. Exploding to feel better is like eating a whole box of low-fat cookies to lose weight.

SLOWING DOWN YOUR ANGER

"Your bike's in great shape. But it could use some new brakes."

We live in Wisconsin, proud home of the Harley-Davidson motorcycle company. Sudden anger is a lot like a Harley—loud, fast, powerful. Sure, the ride's a little wild, but that's the way it's supposed to be. Put on your leathers and take it on the road.

But even Harleys need brakes. It's that or crash and burn.

Slow down. That's what you need to do if you have a sudden anger style. And you can't slow down without a good set of brakes.

You can learn to put on the brakes even if you have a problem with sudden anger. Of course, it's also smart to take your foot off the gas pedal once in a while.

Actually, there are many ways to slow down your anger. Here we'll describe four methods: learning to notice the warning signs that your anger is building, taking a time-out, relaxing, and learning to talk calmly.

Warning Signs

People used to believe that volcanoes just exploded from time to time. But the more scientists studied those volcanoes, the more warning signs they found. Tiny earthquakes. A little smoke. Temperature changes. Now they can predict when an eruption is coming.

People with sudden anger are like volcanoes. Unstudied, they seem to erupt unpredictably. But you can find plenty of danger signs when you take a good look. There are always clues when they're going to erupt.

If you have this anger style, go back to the last time you exploded. What was the last thought you had, right before you blew? Maybe it was "I can't take it anymore," or "they can't do this to me," or "I hate you." Maybe that thought was even, "Boy, am I being patient right now!" What about your feelings? Was your stomach churning, your head splitting, your chest heaving? Or did you tense up and stop breathing? And how about your actions? These might include pacing, making fists, foot bouncing, voice rising (or your voice may have suddenly become very quiet, like the calm before a storm). Are these thoughts, feelings, and actions the ones you usually have right before the storm breaks? If not, what other last signs do you have?

You might want to ask the people you get mad at what signs they see. They can probably tell you. But remember, you're the expert on you. Only you know what you're really thinking, feeling, and doing just before you explode.

Exercise: Now is a good time to make a list of what happens before you get angry. Do it yourself. Ask others who know you to help. Have a friend ask you questions to help you think about it.

First list the physical signs of tension buildup. Some places people commonly experience increased tension are in the head, neck, shoulders, stomach, back, hands, feet, jaw, eyes, chest. What signals do you give yourself?

Now list the mental clues that come before explosion. Some common ones are negative ideas about other people, feeling like a victim, feeling like a saint, thinking that nothing matters, thinking others "deserve" your anger, thinking you can't control yourself. What thoughts come before your explosions?

Finally, list the actions that say you are building up a head of steam. Some people tap their feet, grit their teeth, bite their lips, can't sit, work harder, make fists, walk heavier, pace, or sigh. How do you signal your explosions?

Your first job is to notice these final warning signs. Ignore them and you'll explode in about thirty seconds. Noticing them gives you a choice. You can avoid a blowup now.

"Oh, oh. Here I go again. I'm making fists. My heart is pounding. I'm thinking nobody understands me. I'm gonna blow. I better do something fast."

Later, after you've learned to recognize these signs, you can learn earlier signs. Then you'll be better able to stay calm. But let's keep things simple for now. All you need are your last thought, feeling, and action.

Time-out

You're so mad you can't think straight. This is no time for discussion. You have to get away. You need a time-out.

Time-outs aren't complicated. But there are a few guidelines to make them work well.

Tell people in advance that you're trying something new. Then they won't be surprised when you call a time-out. They won't think you're just running away or punishing them by not talking. And, hopefully, they won't chase after you trying to continue the argument.

Follow these Four R's to have a good time-out:

- *Recognize.* Know the build-up signs that you are losing control over your anger.

- *Retreat.* Get out before you say or do something that you'll regret.

- *Relax.* Do things that help you relax such as taking a quiet walk, reading a book, meditating. You'll know it's working when you feel the anger draining from your body and being replaced with feelings of calmness, serenity, and peace of mind.

- *Return.* That means going back after you calm down with a willingness to discuss the issue from a problem-solving perspective. "How can we fix this problem?" not "Who is at fault here?" is the key to ending conflicts on a positive note.

So first look for the signs you are about to blow. What do you think, feel, say, and do right before you explode? You know you're in trouble when you have these thoughts and feelings, so use them for something useful. Let them be the messengers that tell you to take a time-out right now.

It helps to tell your partner that you need to take a time-out. "Helen, I gotta get out of here for a while. I can feel myself getting mad. I'll be back when I cool off." Keep that promise, too. Time-outs are different from refusing to deal with things.

Now go somewhere to relax—your room, your car, a friend's home. Listen to music. Read. Watch TV. Sometimes activity helps, like riding your bike or lifting weights. But be careful about potentially dangerous things like chopping wood. And don't head for the local bar or talk with people who tell you to get more pissed. The idea is to relax, to let that anger drain away. You've got to get back in control.

Then go back. It's time to discuss whatever you were talking about when you got so excited. But stay calm this time.

A time-out can take five minutes or five hours. Don't try to set a rigid limit. It's useless to go back too soon. You'll just get angry all over again. But it's very important to return to the scene of the crime. You've got to learn to discuss things more calmly.

Relaxing

People with sudden anger have a secret enemy—stress. The slow buildup of physical and mental tension, when unrelieved, triggers most sudden explosions, especially the ones that seem to come from nowhere.

Relaxation reduces stress. You can stop most of your explosions before they begin by training yourself to relax.

Don't wait until the last second, though. You can't make yourself relax by sheer willpower, not when you're already tearing your hair out. By then it's too late. It's frustrating and useless to say, "I'm gonna relax, right now, before I scream. Now breathe, breathe, breathe. Oh what's the use. I'm so anxious I can't relax. This isn't working."

People with sudden anger can benefit greatly from stress reduction training. You can get that through books, therapy, and biofeedback exercises. Here, though, are a few tips that can help you get started:

- *Start with your face.* That's the part of you that you are most used to controlling, so it's the easiest place to gain quick control when you need it. Begin by letting your eyes soften, then loosen your chin and jaw, then the area around your mouth, then your temples and the rest of your face.

- *Breathe slowly and deeply.* Feel the good air going into your lungs. Let go of tension, frustration, anger, and anxiety as you exhale. Take at least ten full breaths.

- *Make yourself talk with your normal voice.* That usually means getting quieter and speaking more slowly. Remember the tone of your voice tells both yourself and others what you are feeling.

- *Calm your body down.* Sit down if you're pacing. Unclench those fists. Quit tapping your feet. Loosen those tight muscles that are causing your back or gut to ache. Breathe.

- *Tell yourself to relax.* You'll need a few messages that you'll listen to at the moment of truth, such as: "Come on, relax. It's not the end of the world." Or: "I have a choice here. I don't have to blow. Just relax." Breathe.

Calm Talk

Talking calmly is about as easy for exploders as climbing trees is for dogs. It doesn't come naturally. Standing up and yelling, on the other hand, that's natural. So is screaming at the top of their lungs. Swearing a blue streak. Crying jags. Unfortunately, those actions cause trouble. There's nothing worse than having a natural talent at something nobody appreciates.

Breathe. Calmness is both an attitude and a set of behaviors. You can learn each.

The attitude is this: "I intend to stay calm, no matter what. That doesn't mean trying to stay calm. It means staying calm, no matter what. I'm tired of acting like a two-year-old when I get upset. I'm ready to grow up and stay grown up. No more excuses." Breathe.

You need to make a solid promise to yourself. To succeed, you must make a total commitment to giving up angry outbursts. Alcoholics Anonymous has a useful slogan: "Half measures avail us nothing." A halfhearted effort won't work because the temptation to blow off steam can get awfully strong. Breathe.

More than an attitude, calmness is also a set of simple and clear actions:

- Sit down.

- Speak quietly.

- Don't swear.

- Talk slowly.

- Listen to what others say.

- Breathe fully and evenly.

- Don't jump to conclusions.

- Don't exaggerate.

- Solve problems.

You'll need to practice these behaviors. They may not come naturally, but they will come if you work at it. And you'll find that they get easier with practice, just like any new skill. Breathe.

6

Shame-based Anger

A few years ago we wrote a book called *Letting Go of Shame*. We began with a story about a little girl who finds a special place in her garden. There she digs happily in the soft soil. She feels great about what she's doing. "Look at me," she tells her mom. "Look at what I can do."

"Just look at you!" shouts her mother. "You've made a mess. Your clothes are ruined. You're so dirty. You should be ashamed of yourself."

The little girl feels bad, and small, and weak. She drops her head. She cries. She feels ugly and dirty inside. She thinks there must be something awfully bad about her, something so terrible she'll never really be clean again. She feels damaged, broken.

People we talked with brought up that little girl again and again. Grown men and women told us they were just like her. They too felt lousy about themselves. They felt bad and weak and damaged and small. They felt ashamed.

Shame is the painful sense of feeling defective as a human being.

Shame has many parts. Shamed people often blush with embarrassment. Their head bows down as if someone were pushing on their neck. Eye contact feels impossible. It's hard to talk. Their gut suddenly churns. Some people feel nauseated as they literally become sick with their shame.

People think terrible things about themselves when they're ashamed. Some of these thoughts are: "I am worthless," "I am nothing," "Nobody loves me," "I am weak," "I am bad," "I can't do anything right."

Meanwhile, it's hard to take positive action. Most people just want to run away and hide when they feel shame. If they can't actually leave, they quit talking or doing things. Shame often paralyzes people, freezing them in their tracks.

Shame also can bring on a spiritual crisis. People who are deeply ashamed wonder if they belong anywhere. They don't seem to fit in very well. They sometimes wonder if they are a mistake. They may doubt that their lives have any value or meaning. They start to believe they are subhuman, less than fully alive. They feel empty, drained of spirit.

Shame is a powerful and complicated emotion. Sometimes it has value. Shame can point the way to healthy pride. For instance, someone who flunks a test because he didn't study may feel some shame about that. That's good shame if he then studies harder for the next test. If shame were a coin, its flip side would be pride, honor, dignity, and self-respect.

Shame is like anger. A little is good but too much is bad. And some people have way too much shame. We call them shame-based, because their lives center around shame. They are also shame-bound because shame ties them up in knots made from feelings of being bad, different, and not good enough.

SHAME AND RAGE

Merle's a great guy, except for one thing. He's way too sensitive about his looks. Yesterday, for instance, his wife Tammy kidded him about his weight. She patted his belly after a big meal and chuckled a little. Merle wasn't amused. He felt insulted. "Why'd you do that, Tammy? Are you saying I'm fat? You're not exactly skinny yourself, you know.

And that dress you're wearing is really gross." The more he thought about it, the angrier he got. He kept after her all night, making her pay for the mean thing she said. Because he felt ashamed, he spent all evening dumping shame on her.

Shame is not exactly a fun emotion. It takes great courage, and sometimes years of therapy or recovery, to tackle shame head-on. Instead, many people figure out ways to avoid dealing with their shame.

Getting away (withdrawal) is the most common defense against shame. Other defenses include denial ("Ashamed? About what? I don't feel bad about anything"); arrogance (pretending to be better than others when you really feel worse); addiction; and perfectionism ("If I can only be perfect I won't have anything to feel ashamed about").

One more very common defense against shame is anger. This is a special kind of anger, though. Its technical name is *narcissistic rage*. This is extremely strong anger that gets triggered when the person starts to feel personally attacked, like Merle, above.

Janette is another example. She can't stand criticism at work. Last week her coworker Diana suggested a new way to keep track of sales. That's Janette's turf. She took Diana's remarks as a personal attack. You could almost see the steam rising. Janette ran off crying, but not before she told Diana she was a stupid bitch who had better keep her nose out of Janette's business. That earned a visit from her boss, and a written reprimand.

Merle and Janette are full of shame. Their self-concepts are low. They don't like themselves very much, and it shows.

Why these rages? Because shame-bound people are extremely defensive. It's as if their self-worth is a glass house and everybody's throwing rocks. The only way they can protect their house is to throw bigger rocks. So they end up attacking, trying to destroy the other person's self-worth first. "I'll show you," they think. "I'll make you feel like dirt because that's what you think of me."

Shame-bound people think they are pretty crummy excuses for human beings. They're certain others don't like them because they despise themselves. But shame isn't something people advertise. Nobody wears a T-shirt that reads, "Look at me. I belong to the Pond Scum Society."

Rage keeps others away from that central feeling of badness. The rager is shouting a warning: "Don't get any closer. You are getting too near my shame, and I won't let you see that part of me. Stay away or I will attack."

Rage works. It does drive people away. You can bet that Merle's wife and Janette's coworkers will think twice before saying anything again. Rage keeps people at a safe distance. It protects deeply shamed people from anybody getting close enough to see their shame. But sometimes it works too well. Ragers become isolated. Nobody dares get close because they get punished too often. "Sure, I like Merle. But he gets so mad over little things." Or, "I just wish Janette would quit being so sensitive." That only makes the shame-bound person feel worse, of course. It's hard to feel good about yourself when others avoid you. So a person's shame fuels their anger, and their anger drives people away, and then they feel even more shameful. They feel lonelier, too.

Exercise: A word or an action can be negative, positive, or neutral. When you are shame-bound, you see neutral words and events as negative. Often you even think a positive comment is a criticism. For the next month, every time you feel criticized by someone else's word or action, *stop.* Breathe. Then ask them if what they said or did was meant to be critical, if it was just something they said or did without a bad motive (neutral), or if it was positive.

Because you judge yourself harshly, you think others do, too. Some might. But many may not. You really don't have good judgment here. Check things out. Check things out again. Learn the difference between a comment and a criticism. Learn the difference between someone concentrating and someone ignoring you. Turn the volume down on your shame-based reaction.

THE FIVE WORST THINGS PEOPLE SAY TO THEMSELVES

Shame-bound people say five negative messages to themselves. These five self-criticisms lead to the rages we've been describing. These are the phrases:

- I'm no good.

- I'm not good enough.

- I don't belong.

- I'm not lovable.

- I should not be.

I'm No Good

Rotten to the core. Useless. Worthless. That's what this message is about. When you believe you are no good you feel utterly hopeless. How can you change when you think you are totally bad? You're sure anyone would reject you if they got to know you well. Others would say, "Ugh, who wants her? She's awful. She's so ugly inside. She's no good for anything."

Ragers who think this way are full of self-hatred. They certainly don't want others around. So they play keep away. "Keep away from me. I'm no good. If you try to get close I'll make you feel no good too." Sometimes they are depressed, and they may need some treatment for depression. Often they have been told that they were no good since they were small. For example, Doug got scared by the way his parents fought. Soon, whenever they were starting to have a fight, he would do something he wasn't supposed to. It would stop the fight, at least temporarily. His parents told him he was no good because they couldn't make him "behave." But really, his "no goodness" came from trying to stop his parents' fighting. He still thinks that he is no good, but that is not true.

I'm Not Good Enough

Will's never satisfied with himself. Whatever he does is not quite good enough. The chicken he grilled should have been tastier. He could have sold another couple cars this month. Having sex was nice, but he should have been able to delay coming a few more minutes.

Sandra specializes in comparisons. She's not as good as Howard at graphics. She's worse at raising kids than her sister. And her figure just isn't good enough to attract men. Sandra's convinced that she would always finish fourth in the Olympics. Good try but no medal.

Many people believe they're not good enough. Sometimes they tell others, sometimes it's their hidden secret. They may actually be very good at what they do. But that makes little difference. They feel like losers. They try hard, though. If only they could do something completely right, they say to themselves, maybe this horrible sense of inadequacy would vanish. They often become perfectionists, trying to do everything exactly right. If only they could, then they'd feel no shame. Or that is what they think. Unfortunately, though, human beings aren't designed to be perfect. Failures happen to everyone.

Especially to perfectionists. Why do more failures happen to them? Because they can always find some reason that what they have done is not perfect, even if everyone else thinks it's wonderful.

Failure is very painful when you're full of shame. That goes double when someone else calls attention to your faults. "How dare you criticize me!" they say. "You have no right. Besides, you're not so great yourself. You're not as smart as Shelly."

I Don't Belong

Draw a circle. Put a dot in the center of it. This circle stands for all the places people belong. The circle of your birth family. The circle of your current household. The circles of work, and friendships, and school, and church. Now place an X where you belong.

People who believe they don't belong put themselves on the edge of the circle, sometimes with one foot in and one foot out. Or they mark their X completely outside the circle. "I've never felt I belong anywhere," they tell us. They've always felt like outsiders. It's as if they can never join the club, never get on the bus. They're different, and bad.

"I'm different, I don't belong" feels horrible. It just plain hurts.

What if someone happens to say or do something that triggers those feelings of being different? Disaster. "You think it's funny I like serious movies instead of comedies? Go to hell! I'll watch whatever I want." Alone.

I'm Not Lovable

Ask someone who is feeling unlovable how old they feel right then. They usually answer, "three" or "five" or "very young." They first felt unloved as a child. But feeling unloved is like getting bitten by a bulldog. It's hard to shake off.

Some families promote shame more than others. The phrase "I love you" is seldom heard in these families. The result is that children grow up thinking they're not special, important to others, or worth loving. They feel unwanted. They believe they'll never be deeply loved by another human being.

Also, parents may suddenly withdraw their love, or threaten to do so. "Wilma, if you don't do what I want, I won't love you anymore." They may also reject their children by turning away or giving them the silent treatment. These acts and threats are terrifying to children, who depend on their parents for physical survival and emotional support. Without love, they fear they'll be abandoned.

As adults, deeply shamed people still fear abandonment. This is doubly true for those who think they're unlovable. No matter how long and well someone loves them, they just can't believe it will last. They always have their mental bags packed, expecting their partners and friends to reject them.

It's hard to live in fear. That's where shame-based anger comes in. Why not attack first? Why not reject others before they get a chance to discard you? Tell them you don't love them anymore. Refuse to speak with them for days at a time. Give them the cold shoulder. Make them hurt for loving you, like you hurt for loving your parents. Always be sure they need you more than you need them.

Feeling unlovable, people become unloving. Fearing abandonment, they become abandoners.

I Should Not Be

Juliet, a young woman just out of school, has a good job and a steady relationship. But she is full of pessimism. "What's the use?" she asks. "Why bother? I wish I had never been born."

"I should not be." This is the worst shame message of all. People who think this way get depressed. They feel totally hopeless and full of despair. Empty. They can't find any meaning in their lives.

Deeply shamed people often feel this despair. Their lives don't seem to have any value. They've lost interest in themselves. They have no curiosity, no sense of wonder.

People who believe they should not be can get very angry. Their rage goes in two directions. Self-harm is one path. After all, why take care of themselves when their life is worthless? Deeply shamed people are experts at self-neglect, self-abuse, and self-reproach. And they may try to kill themselves. Why go on living when they are a mistake in the first place?

Their anger can also be directed at others. Then it often takes the form of neglect or contempt. The shamed person simply refuses to recognize another's existence. "You aren't worth noticing" is the message. "You don't even exist." Last week Steve told Pam he loved her. He said he wanted to live with her forever. Today he moved out while Pam was at work and left without a note. Pam doesn't matter anymore. She means nothing to Steve.

SHAME AND BLAME IS THE NAME OF THE GAME

Shame and blame are natural partners. The worse people feel, the more likely they are to take the blame for anything that goes wrong. And, when people turn the tables and start shaming others, the weapon they use is blame.

Penny and Becky are lovers. At least that's what they call their relationship. Their friends have nicknamed them the Hellcats, though, because all they do is fight. They're always bickering. They nitpick each other, constantly finding fault. And then they really attack. They bloody each other with their sharp tongues. Worst of all, they try to humiliate each other in public. They are one mean couple.

This is a two-way shame and blame relationship. The goal is to defeat the other person. The weapons are shame and blame. Victory comes when one of them makes the other feel like the poorest excuse for a human being that ever walked on earth.

Two-way shame and blame relationships can go on for years. They're balanced. Both persons know how to hurt the other badly. Both do so regularly. These relationships look like old-time bare-knuckled brawls. "All right, ladies and gentlemen. It's time for round 144. Come out fighting." Each partner feels powerful in victory, miserable in defeat. Neither knows how to change things. They only know how to fight. Shame and blame is the name of their game.

Jeff and Melinda have a one-way shame and blame relationship. Jeff is the only shamer/blamer. No matter what Melinda does, he criticizes her. She's never good enough for him. The longer this goes on, the weaker she feels. Slowly, criticism by criticism, he's gaining power.

Shaming and blaming another is a deliberate way to gain power. People gain control by shaming others. For example, Jeff tells Melinda she's unattractive, that she's so ugly no other man would want her. She feels ugly when he says that. She starts to take less care of herself and is told she's even worse looking. The worse she feels, the worse she looks. Now she's grateful he even keeps her, since she's so plain. She feels more and more ashamed. She'll do anything he says now, because she's afraid he'll discard her and no other man will want her.

One-way shame increases power differences over time. Two people who started out nearly equal won't stay that way if one gains control of the shame process. The shamer/blamer will gradually become more powerful.

SHAME, RAGE, AND EMPTINESS

Debbie grew up in a family in which nobody seemed to care much about anybody else. Debbie even wondered, when she was young, if her parents would remember her birthday. Sometimes they did, but not always. She seldom felt special or wanted.

Debbie's an adult now. She feels empty inside. It's a terrible emptiness, a bottomless pit of loneliness. She tries to fill up that hole inside her, but nothing works. Every day she feels an aching void at the very center of her being.

Last year Debbie began dating Douglas, another empty and unhappy person. Each wants the other to care for them. Both need to be filled up emotionally. But how can they give to each other what they don't have themselves? At first their neediness brought them together. But now they are driving each other crazy by asking for so much.

"Pay attention to me. Always." That's what Debbie demands.

"Do you really love me?" Doug asks ten times a day.

Both are watchful, jealous, suspicious. They never feel really safe with each other. Sooner or later, they figure, the other one will leave them. No amount of reassurance works, either. Debbie tells Doug she loves him over and over, but he keeps doubting. Doug comes home early almost every night, but Debbie still fears he won't come home at all.

Debbie and Doug are asking the impossible. They want their partner to fill their emptiness. No one can do that.

Debbie and Doug fight a lot. Each feels a desperate rage. They demand total loyalty. Both want to guarantee their love by taking away the other's freedom. They dread abandonment. "I can't live without you" is their theme. Soon they're battling all the time. "Stay with me forever. Fill my emptiness. I'll hate you if you don't."

Debbie and Doug do love each other. But their shame keeps getting in the way. They just feel too worthless and unlovable. They are so worried about being abandoned they cannot relax. They can't take in a little love at a time. Could a starving man settle for a crumb of bread? They demand total love, perfect love. But perfect love is impossible.

These two will need to work on their shame issues. If not, they will lose each other. Their love will turn into bitter disappointment, and then into hate.

SHAME-BASED ANGER CAN BE STOPPED

Shame-based anger comes on fast. But, unlike sudden anger, it goes away slowly. That's because the exploder usually feels worse and more ashamed after an outburst than before. Shame clings like lint on an old suit, and all the anger in the world can't seem to pull it off.

You can lower the number of shame/rage episodes by doing three things. First you have to break the shame/rage connection so you don't take out your shame on others. Next you must begin to heal your shame, and then you must treat others with respect, the opposite of shame.

Breaking the Shame/Rage Connection

Shame is bad enough. It's worse when you turn it into rage. Now you've got two problems instead of one.

The link is simple enough. When you start to feel ashamed, you get mad. Better to attack than be attacked. Shame them first, shame them more. Scare them off. Then maybe they'll leave you alone.

Why change? Because you'll never feel good about yourself this way. You'll win a few battles by making others feel even worse than you for a while. But you'll still feel lousy about yourself. Shaming and attacking others may hide your shame, but it won't heal it.

You'll need some personal information to change. What do people say or do that triggers your shame? When does this happen? With whom? In what situations? How often?

How do you convert shame into anger? By shouting at anyone who dares criticize you? By putting people down? Do you get nasty when people expect too much? Do you become cynical or sarcastic? Do you nitpick?

The best way to break the shame/rage link is to ask yourself one question every time you get angry: "What am I ashamed about right now?" Okay, maybe you're not ashamed every time you get angry. But it won't hurt to ask the question. That's how you can use your anger as a signal to deal with your shame.

Watch for sudden bursts of anger. They often signal hidden shame. Somebody says something critical that catches you by surprise. Before you know it you're yelling at them. You feel wounded, as if you had been stabbed in the back. You feel hurt, abandoned, betrayed. Your rage tells them you're mightily pissed. But it can tell you that they've touched your shame and that's why you're so angry.

Sometimes you feel shame because another person wants to shame you. They really are saying nasty things to you or about you. But remember this: People don't sit around all day figuring out ways to shame you. They've got better things to do. Many times, when you feel suddenly attacked and shamed, it's you who is ashamed of yourself. But it's easier to blame others than to accept responsibility. If it's your shame, then it's you who has to change, not them.

Now you've identified the shame/rage link. But there's one more thing to do. You've got to commit to breaking the link. That means altering your behavior. You have to stop the anger *now*. Take a time-out if you need one. If you can, tell the other person you're having a shame attack and you need to talk about it. Don't give in to your anger. It's a distraction from your real feelings. The main issue is your shame.

Healing Your Shame

We mentioned earlier that shame can be good. Healthy shame comes in small doses. It only lasts a short time. It tells you what to do so you can feel better about yourself. That means the goal isn't to get rid of all shame. It's to reduce shame to a manageable level.

Shame is like a Minnesota winter. No matter how much you shovel, you know the snow will return. You have to work hard to reduce your shame, and you have to keep working at it. But don't get discouraged. Spring does come, even in Minnesota.

Shame heals slowly. You'll know you're doing better when you believe five statements most of the time:

- I am good.

- I am good enough.

- I am lovable.

- I belong.

- I am.

Take a look at these messages. Which do you most need? Which would help you be less defensive or angry? Select just one for starters.

Can you put the message in your own words? For example: "I am good enough" might be "I do my work well. I don't need to make excuses." Or: "I belong" could be "I fit in. There's room for me in this world." Take a minute to absorb the message. Feel it in your gut.

How could your life change to honor that message? What must you say or do differently? Do you need to be more assertive? Hold your head higher? Take pride in what you do? Quit apologizing? Finish what you begin? Do more things with your family or friends? Take in praise? Be less sensitive to criticism? Do you just need to let yourself be?

Shame gradually turns into self-respect and healthy pride. But only if you change your thoughts and actions.

There's something else that helps heal shame. Put nonshaming people in your life.

Shame is the great isolator. It shoves people into little corners of the world. So, if you want to heal your shame, you'll have to come out of the corner. You just can't heal all your shame by yourself. You need to share your whole self, even the parts of you that feel bad. But make sure you find people who will help you feel better about yourself, not worse. People who don't need to find fault with you. They also need to be honest with you, though, because you change best when you face the truth.

Look around. You may need to get professional help, but don't forget about friends and family. There are a lot of good people in this world, but you need to find them.

Treating Others with Respect

We wrote earlier about shaming and blaming relationships. Here one or both partners constantly attack each other, trying to make the other feel totally bad, stupid, worthless, and weak.

Shaming and blaming have got to go. There's no room for this stuff in good relationships. Shaming and blaming make everybody feel worse. The shamed person feels terrible, of course. But the shamers don't exactly come out of the mud with clean boots, either. They're only showing people how bad they really feel about themselves. They could wear a sign that reads, "Look at me. I hate myself. I'm just trying to make you feel as bad as I do."

Below you will find a list of ways to treat others with respect. Ron made this list for his book *Angry All the Time*, and it's worth repeating here.

The goal is to get the shaming and blaming out of your relation-ships. You can begin by choosing one or two items from the Don't list to stop. For instance, if you're always looking for things to criticize, tell yourself to quit. Instead, start noticing things to praise. It won't be easy, of course. It's like learning to look at the sky when all your life you've been staring at the ground. But it's worth it.

Maybe you shame others by ignoring them. You act like they're not even there. So make a personal promise to quit ignoring them. Then really take the time to listen, to take interest, to care. It's tempting to go back to reading the newspaper or watching TV. But stick with it. You'll probably find that people pay more attention to you when you show interest in them.

Exercise: Below the Dos and Don'ts is a set of questions you may want to copy. Use them to understand your shame-based anger. They can help you change the way you take out your anger on others.

When you find yourself feeling angry, ask yourself these six questions. If you can, sit down and take the time to write out the answers. Shame is sneaky, and it's easy to forget what really happened. If you write the answers out, you will have them to refer to another time.

1. Is this anger a signal that I might have some shame about something?

2. If I weren't feeling anger right now, what would I be feeling? Any of the following are danger signals that this anger could be shame-based: empty, bored, embarrassed, exposed, inadequate, vulnerable, disliking something in myself.

3. Who could I talk to about this? Who would be least likely to reject me or attack me when they knew I wasn't feeling okay about myself? Could I ask them to help me look at myself and not support my anger right now?

4. How can I deal with the other person respectfully, without dumping on them because I am feeling bad about myself?

5. How can I take care of myself better? What are the cues for my inadequate, embarrassed, or threatened feelings? What could I do when I start noticing them other than getting mad at other people?

6. What do I need to do to respect myself right now? How can I affirm and reward myself for doing the right thing?

Dos and Don'ts
for Treating Others with Respect

Do:

- begin each day with a promise to respect others
- sit down and talk quietly
- listen carefully to what others say
- look for things to appreciate in others
- give praise out loud for the good you see in others
- tell others they are good, good enough, and lovable
- tell others they are worthwhile and important to you
- speak in a quiet voice even when you disagree
- pass up chances to insult, attack, or criticize
- let others have responsibility for their lives while you take responsibility for yours

Don't:

- look for things to criticize
- make fun or laugh at others
- make faces or roll your eyes
- tell others how to run their lives
- insult others
- ignore others
- put people down in front of others
- act superior
- sneer
- tell others they're weird or crazy
- say others are bad, not good enough, or unlovable
- say others don't belong, or you wish they were dead
- call others names like fat, ugly, stupid, or worthless

7

Deliberate Anger

Amanda is a holy terror. She rants and raves whenever she doesn't get what she wants. She instantly flies off the handle. Her family's afraid of her. Her coworkers avoid her as much as they can. Amanda seems to be a classic rageaholic.

But Amanda's a fake. She tells us in counseling that she's hardly ever really very angry. "Come on, Pat," she says. "You know I'm not that angry. Hey, I'd be in the hospital if I were. I'd blow a gasket. Sure, I'm a little pissed. But it's mostly a show."

What a show! Amanda deliberately exaggerates her anger. She wants people to think she could go crazy with her anger any minute.

ANGER, THE PHONY OR EXAGGERATED EMOTION

Some people just plain fake their anger almost all the time. Here's an example. Ron was teaching a psychology class at a local college. One day he discovered nobody had read anything. He got angry. He felt his temperature rising. He didn't want to make a scene, though, so he marched out of the room, telling the students to come back tomorrow knowing something about the topic.

Ron heard footsteps behind him as he walked away. They followed him right to his office. They belonged to a twenty-year-old student named Victor. Ron asked him what he wanted.

"Good job, Ron," Victor said. "You looked like you were actually angry."

"Well, that was easy, Victor, because I was angry."

"You were? Honestly? Gee, I'm never really mad. I always just pretend."

What's going on here? Why do people exaggerate or fake being angry? The answer is simple. Some people have learned that anger works. They can get what they want, when they want it, by pretending to get mad. After all, anger is scary. Who wants to mess with someone who is really pissed off? "Just let her have what she wants," people say.

If you get angry a lot, ask yourself this question: "What do I gain when I get mad?" What are the payoffs? You won't be able to quit being angry so much until you know what the secret benefits are.

We'll describe four main payoffs for anger. These are the main reasons why some people deliberately work up a rage:

- Power—to make others do what you want

- Image—to show off or look good

- Distance—to keep others away

- Emotional control—to avoid real feelings

Power

Joe goes crazy whenever he doesn't get his way. Edith flies into a rage if her husband doesn't come home on time. Bill storms around the office, terrifying his assistants. Mary grumbles for hours if her parents won't let her go out. Each swears they can't help it. "That's just the way I am," they say.

Each of these people has a secret, though. They really could control their temper, but they don't want to. They like the results too much. They think things like, "I like to scare people with my anger. Besides, that's how I get what I want. Nobody messes with me when I blow up." They also think things like:

"I'll show her who's the boss."

"He'd *better* do what I want."

"It's my way or else."

Most people don't like getting angry very often. The strong feelings are upsetting. Besides, they might do something they'll regret. They're afraid of losing control.

But what if it just looks like you're losing control? Actually, you know exactly what you're doing. You're throwing things around (just their things, not yours). You're threatening to beat someone up. You're almost foaming at the mouth. All the time, though, you're totally aware. You're alert. You know exactly what you want. You enjoy yourself during the show. And once you get what you want, or scare people well enough so you think you'll get what you want for a long time, your anger's over.

Neil Jacobsen, a well-known psychologist, and his colleagues did research on male batterers. They discovered that some of the worst batterers didn't get emotionally upset as they fought with their wives. Instead, their heart rates dropped as they got angry. They became calmer, not more agitated. Jacobsen concluded that these men got violent on purpose. Their violence was designed to control their wives through fear. Their fury was paired with cool control.

These men weren't only angry and violent toward their spouses. They took on other family members, friends, coworkers, just about anybody. They tried to get what they wanted by scaring people.

Power. That's what we're talking about. Getting what you want by overwhelming others. The basic message is "I want what I want, and I want it now." Intimidation. "They won't dare defy me. I can make them do what I want" by yelling, pouting, fighting, and maybe hitting.

This is deliberate anger. It's not about feelings. It's about power. And it's dangerous, because sometimes it's accompanied by a power rush. People who use deliberate anger sometimes find themselves enjoying hurting someone else. "Faking it" turns into a power rush, and they hurt others just to hurt them, to feel even more powerful and in control. They tell us when this happens, "There's a bad side to me that comes out, and I don't feel in control of who I am anymore." They lose the very thing they started out to achieve, a sense of control.

Deliberate anger often works its way down the chain of command in a family. The biggest or most powerful person bosses the next strongest, who bosses the next one down, and so on. The littlest one kicks the dog, or fights with other kids to get power. Each one teaches the next one how to be angry to get what they want.

Nobody gives up power willingly. That's doubly true for people who use deliberate anger to gain power. They seldom volunteer to quit getting angry on purpose. It's pretty useless to try to get them to "just say no" to their anger. They usually won't change until their anger gets them into a lot of trouble. They need consequences, not therapy.

Some deliberately angry people use other feelings to manipulate people, too. They may be good at getting other people to feel sorry for them, thus avoiding consequences for their behavior. They can put on a puppy-dog look just as quickly and just as falsely as they do anger. Feeling sorry for them after they have been mean, though, is a *big* mistake. They need consequences. They need to learn that faking anger and being mean to get power is not okay and will not work for them anymore.

Deliberately angry people need to look at their lives honestly. We will talk about how to do that later in this chapter. If you are good at being deliberately angry to get power, read the sections beginning with "Saying Good-Bye to an Old Friend." You will learn about a different kind of power. You will discover a new way to respect yourself. Others will respect you a lot more, too. Power has limits you never thought about before.

Image

He's rough. He's tough. He never bluffs. He's macho man. Image is the desire to impress others by looking and acting tough. Everybody plays roles: husband, mother, teacher, dancer. The roles tell us and other people what we do. They say a little bit about who we are.

One role is "tough guy." Both men and women can be tough guys. And, like all roles, there are rules and expectations.

Tough guy rule 1: The only feeling you can show is anger. That's it. Any displays of other feelings, especially fear, are strictly prohibited.

Tough guy rule 2: Cause trouble, or stomp on trouble. Never run away from a fight. In fact, always wade into battle. The bigger they are, the better chance to show you're not afraid of anybody.

Tough guy rule 3: Use your anger to keep people away. Don't get close to others. Don't make emotional connections. Falling in love is like sitting in a restaurant with your back to the door. You're gonna get ambushed. Avoid it at all costs. Don't trust anybody.

Tough guy rule 4: If you aren't really mad, fake it. Remember, this is about image. The tough guy has to look that way at all times.

There are a lot of tough guys in this world. Most of them grew up in angry families, dangerous neighborhoods. They really are tough, so playing the role comes easy. And they're good at what they do.

If you're a tough guy, you value your image. You want others to see you as strong and powerful. You look for reasons to get mad, because each fight gives you a chance to show off your toughness. You get mad on purpose.

It's easy to develop a reputation as a hothead or rebel. The hard part is getting out of the role.

Here's an example. Twenty-year-old Al has a reputation for being thin-skinned. He's always getting into fights over stuff others would ignore. He claims to be terribly insulted if someone ignores him, or if they say something wrong. Then he challenges them to fight. He wins most of these battles because he's quick with his hands.

Al liked being known as a fighter for a long time. Truth is, he wasn't all that angry. But he thought others feared and respected him because he was so dangerous. Then one day he discovered he was being set up. People would tell him things just to piss him off. When he blew up, they'd all come around to watch the show. So Al had to realize he was a fool. He was getting beat up for nothing. Sure, he had a "tough guy" reputation—a "stupid tough guy" reputation.

But Al isn't dumb. He was just hanging onto his image. He didn't think anybody would like him if he quit acting tough. He didn't know who he would be if he wasn't tough all the time. It took all his courage to give up his image, but he finally decided that there was more to life than playacting.

Distance

"Keep away from me." That's one message people deliberately send with their anger.

Anger is the great distancer. You can drive people out of your life with anger. Sometimes they come back. Sometimes they don't.

Here's what the deliberate distancer says: "We had a fight, a big fight. That's when I realized I needed some space. That's why I left the house and stayed away for a couple days."

Here's what really happened. "Well, Ron, I just needed space. We were getting too close. He was starting to talk about love. Next thing he'd want is a commitment. So I picked a huge fight with him. Then I got the hell out of there."

Cause and effect. The deliberate distancer claims the fight causes the need for distance. But it's the other way around. His or her need for distance causes the fight.

Closeness is scary, especially if you've been jilted, abandoned, betrayed, or cheated on. So you decide never to let anybody in. But it's hard to be truthful about that. Your partner might leave you if you tell them that you like them a little, but, by God, you're never in a hundred years going to let them get really close. That would be way too honest.

Enter deliberate anger. Find something, anything, to argue about. Nag. Complain. Grumble. And then explode. Get into fight after fight. The goal is to keep your partner at arm's length. The need is to avoid intimacy. The danger is being vulnerable.

Most of the time the message is "go away for a while. Then I'll let you come back, as long as you don't get too close. If you do, I'll just have to start another brawl." This way, you stay in complete control of the relationship.

But beware. You can only send that message so often. Sooner or later, others will hear the real message: "Get lost. I will never make a real commitment. I refuse to love you." Then they'll leave. You'll be stuck, all alone with your anger. Of course, then you can tell yourself that those no-good SOBs always leave you anyhow. All the more reason to pick fights with the next idiot who tries to love you.

Emotional Control

Helen never learned to cry when she was a child. "Honey," her mother would say, "it's a cruel world out there. Don't ever let them know they've hurt you. Don't ever let them see you cry."

So what does Helen do when she feels sad? She shouts. She fights. She attacks. She does anything so others won't discover her real feelings. She won't let anyone see her soft side, not even herself.

Like many people, Helen uses anger to avoid other feelings. It's not okay for her to feel sad. Similarly, "tough guys" get angry instead of scared. Shame-based people cover their shame with anger. Other people think they aren't supposed to feel lonely or guilty. And still others tell themselves that anger is the only legitimate feeling they can have.

These people share a common theme. They may look out of control when they get mad. But they feel in control. At least they feel more in control than when they have those other feelings.

Anger can be a cover emotion, like a blanket you throw over your other feelings. Nobody knows what's under the blanket. And they won't, as long as you can scream, shout, and yell enough to keep them from taking a peek.

If you use anger to avoid other feelings, you're like the tough guy who secretly loves little kids. You're afraid to let others know because they might laugh. They might take advantage of you. So you never visit children. You don't have any of your own. And once in a while, you wonder why you feel a little empty.

The Costs of Deliberate Anger

Deliberate anger means choosing to get angry—for power, image, distance, and emotional control. It often works. But what are the costs?

Wanda and Wally are cleaning the junk out of their house. "Hey, I've got a great idea," says Wanda. "Let's make a bonfire. We'll burn this stuff up." And they do. Unfortunately, though, they build their fire too close to their home. They forget to keep a few buckets of water. And the wind's blowing about forty miles an hour. Good-bye, house.

Deliberately angry people are like Wanda and Wally. They think they can start a fire and put it out whenever they want. It's not always that simple. Sometimes the fire takes over. That's when it's time for a blind rage.

Ron talked about blind rages in his book *Angry All the Time*. They are the most potent form of anger. The goal in a blind rage is to destroy anyone in your way. Kill or be killed.

Here's how it happens. You can't fake getting angry without looking angry. So you make an angry face, and you raise your voice, and you pace the floor, and you pound the walls. Sure, your head knows it's all a game. But what about your body? It thinks you're in great danger. Your body begins emergency action. So does your limbic system, the older part of your brain responsible for saving your hide when you're in trouble. Together, they flood you with adrenaline. All of a sudden you feel really angry, excited, upset. What started out as fake anger becomes very real, and you explode. Deliberate anger becomes emotional anger. Controlled anger turns into rage. This loss of control is the single greatest danger with deliberate anger.

What about deliberately angry people who never lose control and who use their anger to stay in power? We said earlier that nobody gives up power willingly. That's especially true for intentional rageaholics. But have you considered the long-term costs of what you're doing? How often do your power plays backfire? Have you ever gotten in trouble with the law or ended up in jail? Or lost relationships because the person you thought you could control with your anger got sick of you and took off? Or got so mad you broke your stuff as well as theirs? Or got fired or suspended? Sure, anger is a great weapon. But maybe it's time for you to learn a few new ways to deal with people.

You pay the price of deliberate anger in many other ways: getting trapped in that old tough guy image, getting so good at keeping people away nobody ever gets in, never feeling anything except anger.

Is this how you want to live your life—pretending to be angry when you're not? Hiding your feelings under a blanket of rage? Acting like a grade school bully on the playground of life? If that's not what you want to do with the rest of your life, read on.

SAYING GOOD-BYE TO AN OLD FRIEND

The U-Haul is loaded. The kids are wiggling in the back seat. Your spouse is waiting.

It's time to say a last farewell to your buddy Del Bert A. His full name is Deliberate Anger, but he goes by Del Bert. Or O.P., for On Purpose Anger, his favorite game.

Del Bert sure didn't want you to leave. He fought and argued. He said you'd never make it without him. He reminded you of all the times you got what you wanted by working yourself into a rage. He said you'll regret moving on. He predicted you'll be back very soon, with or without your family. As for being honest with people, Del Bert just laughed. "Go ahead, try it," he scoffed. "Be a wimp. Honesty is for fools."

But you've made up your mind. Sure, you've mastered the art of phony anger. You've used it to get what you want, to keep people away, to be a big shot, to hide feelings. You can fake anger in your sleep. But it's old. Boring. And it doesn't work all that well anymore.

You want more. You want honesty, closeness, a real self instead of an image. And you're willing to work. You're moving on, starting today. Maybe you're ready to grow up a little.

Good-bye, Del Bert. It's time to start over.

Notice the When's, How's, and Why's of Your Deliberate Anger

There's something you need to do before you completely leave the old neighborhood.

Grab a notebook and write down the last couple of times you intentionally got angry. Maybe you completely faked your anger. Perhaps you were a little mad but faked being furious. Record the experience by answering the following questions:

- When did you get deliberately angry? With whom?

- What did you say or do?

- What were the immediate (short-term) results? Did you get what you wanted? Were people scared or angry back at you? Were there any bad things that happened, to you or others?

- What were the long-term results? How did your deliberate anger affect people the next day? Next week? Next month or year?

- What did you hope to gain? Power? Image? Distance? Hiding other feelings? Anything else? Remember, there is always a reason for getting angry on purpose. You need to know your payoffs.

Tell Others

"Oh, no! Tell others about my intentional anger? No way, Pat and Ron. That's like asking a magician to show the audience how he does his best illusions."

Too bad. You gotta do what you gotta do. You gotta come clean.

The Big Book of Alcoholics Anonymous says the only people who can't recover are those who are "constitutionally incapable of being honest." Is that you? If so, maybe you should just skip the rest of this chapter. But if you *can* be honest about your anger, this is the time. You've got to fess up about your dishonest anger in the past as well as make a commitment to stay honest in the present.

Here's how. Ask the two most important people in your life right now—your partner, your child, your friend, your coworker—to meet with you (together if possible). Go through the notes you just made of times when you've faked or exaggerated your anger. Be sure to mention times you've been deliberately angry with each of them. Make your amends. Now take one more step.

Make a Promise

Now you're free from the big lie of deliberate anger. But that's still not enough. What about the future?

You've got to make a promise to tell the truth. No more fake anger. No more exaggerated rages. No more BS. And it's not enough to make a silent promise to yourself. You need witnesses. The best witnesses are those two people you just trusted enough to tell them about your deliberate anger.

For example: "Frank, Brenda, I want to make a promise. From now on I promise to quit faking or exaggerating my anger. Not just with the two of you. With everybody."

Put your promise in writing.

SO WHAT DO I DO WHEN I WANT . . . ?

Your deliberate anger had some uses. It helped you get power, an image, distance, and emotional control. Now what?

How about power? You used to get it by scaring people with anger. Now what? The answer is simple: *Quit trying to control others.* Forget about your wife's weight problem (it wouldn't be a problem if you'd quit grumbling about it). No more blowups to get your boyfriend to take you to the movies. Don't worry. Your girlfriend won't leave you just because she has some friends to spend time with. Your son won't

A Promise to Change

I, _____ (your name), promise to quit faking or exaggerating my anger. Instead, I will tell the truth. I will ask directly for what I want. I won't use my anger to scare or control people.

I give you permission to remind me of this promise at any time you suspect I am faking or exaggerating my anger.

I may get angry in the future. I may tell you I'm angry. If I do, I promise the anger will be real, not phony. And it will not be just to get you or others to do what I want.

Signed _____   Dated _____

Witness _____   Dated _____

Witness _____   Dated _____

go straight to hell by going to that rock concert. Your daughter won't get pregnant just because she wears those slacks or dates that boy you don't like much.

True, you have less "bully power" when you stop using deliberate anger. But so what? You won't need it because you're running your life and letting others run theirs.

There is one more thing you can do, though. Learn to ask for what you want. You don't have to yell, threaten, or shove people around. Just ask. You might not always get what you want, of course. Nobody gets what they want all the time. You need to accept that part of life. Just because you don't get what you want is no excuse for a tantrum, unless you're three years old.

What if you need distance? Try telling people that you need time for yourself. It's best to plan ahead, though. If you want the next weekend off to go bow hunting, you need to talk about it. You might have to compromise a little here and there. But you won't have to pick a fight just to have an excuse to get away.

What if you've been hiding feelings with your anger? Take a deep breath and start talking. Tell others about your fears, loneliness, sadness, joy. Why not? As the saying goes, "If not here, where? If not now, when?" Isn't it time to quit playing games? Feelings are only feelings. They won't kill you by slipping off your tongue.

8

Excitatory Anger

GETTING HIGH AND GETTING HOOKED ON ANGER

"I love the excitement of a fight. That's when I really feel alive."

"Let me tell you a secret, Pat. My rages are intense. They're like sex. A good rage is like having an orgasm."

"I don't feel good arguing all the time with my wife. But I do like the intensity. The adrenaline rush."

"I've lost control. My anger owns me. It's taken over my life."

Anger is often called a negative emotion. It's supposed to be painful. It's supposed to make people anxious, troubled, uncomfortable. Why, then, do some people seek it out? How could anyone get hooked on anger?

The answer is the anger rush.

The anger rush is the strong physical sensation that comes with getting really mad. The rush is the result of the body's natural fight-or-flight response to danger. The surge of adrenaline. The faster heart rate. Quickened breathing. Tensed muscles.

Anger activates the body. The adrenaline boost can help you feel strong. It injects excitement into a dull day. Furthermore, the fight-or-flight message is sent by the limbic system, a more privitive part of the brain responsible for emotions. There's something very primitive and very attractive about letting feelings take over for a while. No more boredom. Who wants to think when you can feel? Who wants to stay in control when your body is ready to explode? Why not go crazy instead?

The anger rush is one of the secret attractions of anger. That burst of energy can be as hard to give up as a cocaine high.

We compare anger to alcohol or drug addiction in this chapter. Specifically, this type of anger is like a stimulant high, the kind people get when they take amphetamines or cocaine. That may seem perfectly natural to some readers, especially those of you who have struggled with other addictions, compulsions, obsessions, and dependencies. The idea also fits because several research studies show that people with alcohol and drug problems often also have serious anger problems. In particular, many people who become chemically dependent have difficulty with impulse control (including impulsive anger) and/or need excessive stimulation to feel normal.

In our first edition of *Letting Go of Anger,* we named this anger style "addictive anger." However, we now believe that "excitatory anger" is a better term. That's because people who get angry this way are primarily seeking excitement and intensity. They may indeed become psychologically addicted during this process, by which we mean they begin depending more and more upon their rages to help them feel energetic, vital, and strong. They may eventually even seek out opportunities for anger, picking fights just so they can sense the strong sensations that they are seeking.

Over time these people will probably become increasingly angry. They will also lose flexibility. Instead of using several anger styles they will depend most often upon excitatory anger, even when that style is a poor choice for the situation. For instance, the man who complains, "We were having a decent discussion when all of a sudden she started yelling and screaming about nothing" may be married to a woman whose need for excitement trumps resolving an issue. When this behavior occurs again and again, it may be reasonable to state that the individual has become addicted to anger.

This pattern, however, is a secondary process that happens only to some people. Others mix up excitatory anger with other anger styles so as not to become dependent upon just one way to respond to anger invitations. Yes, they may enjoy a "good fight" once in a while, but they do not need to argue in order to feel alive and energetic.

Most of the rest of this chapter describes bad things that happen when people rely too much on excitatory anger. Still, this anger style, like all the styles, has positive value. Here are a few of the positive values of excitatory anger:

- *Anger can be stimulating.* Why do people value a "good fight?" Because a healthy conflict brings out the fighter in them. Anyone who has ever watched a high school debate can see that the competition puts a glint in the competitors' eyes and sharpens their thoughts.

- *Intensity is attractive.* To really get into something, even an argument, does feel good. Intensity focuses attention and energizes people.]

- *In relationships, excitatory anger may feel good to one or both partners:* "We know we love each other because we have such strong fights." Of course, people in these relationships tend to live "soap opera" lives, barreling from one crisis to another. But, for some partners, that may feel wonderful and loving.

Since we're talking about anger and addictions in this chapter, here is a useful analogy. Think of excitatory anger as a good but strong liquor, a powerful drink not meant to be used very often. An occasional indulgence of excitatory anger can add intensity and energy to your life. However, it is not smart to use it too often. Becoming dependent upon excitatory anger to feel alive is a serious mistake.

Many problems develop when people begin relying upon excitatory anger. Several of these problems are described next.

Dependence

It's easy to get trapped in anger. When this happens, getting mad becomes the only way a person feels much. People come to need rages so they can feel good, excited, or even alive. They experience loss of control as their anger takes over. They become slaves to their own anger.

Dependence is the main problem with any addiction. Perhaps getting stoned was once a good way to feel less nervous. But now all you think about is marijuana. Maybe gambling was fun, a good way to kill an evening with friends. But now you have to gamble. It's not much fun anymore. In fact, you wish you could stop, and you're scared because you can't. Gambling has taken over your life. The same thing can happen with anger. Once, you could decide when to get mad, and where, and how much. No more. Now your anger decides for you. You are psychologically addicted.

Here we use Craig Nakken's definition of addiction, taken from his book *The Addictive Personality*. Nakken defines addiction as "a pathological (unhealthy) love and trust relationship with an object or event." Events are activities like gambling, shopping, and fighting.

Need for Increased Intensity

The buildup of tolerance is one of the strongest signs of an addiction. The alcoholic must drink more to get a buzz. The gambler needs higher stakes. The same thing happens with excitatory anger. Gradually, anger-addicted people need bigger and bigger fights. At first, a ten-minute argument is plenty exciting. Then they need a half-hour screaming match. Now their fights last hours and include pushing and shoving. Hitting comes next. They need more and more anger, very strong anger, to feel alive. More excitement. More intensity.

Anger-addicted people often mistake intensity for intimacy. They rant and rave, thinking they're showing how much they care. They argue, "If I didn't love you so much I wouldn't get this mad." But they're not showing love. They're really using others. They pick fights because they need intensity and excitement. They're much more in love with their anger than with any person.

AN EXCITATORY ANGER ADDICTION CHECKLIST

Here's a list of questions that will help you find out whether you are addicted to anger.

- ☐ I look for reasons to get angry.

- ☐ I get bored a lot when I'm not angry.

- ☐ I like having a good fight.

- ☐ Sometimes my anger seems to be controlling me.

- ☐ I use anger to avoid other issues in my life.

- ☐ I feel intensely excited in the middle of a fight.

- ☐ I get high from my anger.

- ☐ I get angry more than I used to.

- ☐ My fights keep getting worse—louder, longer, more violent.

- ☐ I make promises to myself to control my anger, but don't keep them.

- ☐ I worry about how much time I spend being angry.

- ☐ I keep looking for things to get angry about.

- ☐ I often feel guilty after I blow up in anger.

- ☐ I feel that I'm addicted to my anger.

Anger is a problem in your life if you check off even one of these statements. You have a serious problem if you check several. The more items you check, the more likely you're psychologically addicted to your anger.

MORE TROUBLE SIGNS

We've noted four main signs of excitatory anger addiction:

- ■ The desire or need to get high from the anger rush

- ■ A buildup of tolerance for anger

- Loss of control

- Mistaking intensity for intimacy in relationships

There are more.

Denial

Margaret's parents, best friend, and fiancé all tell her she has an anger problem. They're very concerned, especially since she lost a job after a fight with her boss. But does she listen? No. She just gets angrier. What right do they have to meddle in her business? She doesn't have an anger problem, she says. Or she wouldn't if those stupid idiots would get out of her way. Margaret is in total denial.

Minimization

Charlie's not much better than Margaret. Sure, he admits he has "a little" anger problem. He gets loud once in a while. No big deal, though. Except that his kids won't talk with him anymore, his wife's suing for divorce, and his best friend quit asking him over to watch football. Charlie's minimizing his anger problem. He admits he has one, but refuses to realize how bad it is.

Rationalization

"Well, Pat, you'd be angry too if you grew up in my family. They were terrible to me. That's why I'm so mean to everybody now." Sorry, but we don't buy it. Who hasn't had a hard time growing up? This person is using his history to justify being irresponsible now. The truth is, he's always looking for excuses to get mad because he wants that anger rush.

Binge Patterns

Some excitatory anger addicts binge on their anger. They don't get angry very often. But when they do, watch out! It's a nonstop rage for hours or days at a time. Nothing else matters. Fight till you drop. Scream till you lose your voice.

Maintenance Patterns

Other excitatory anger addicts prefer a steady daily supply of anger. They get mad every day, but not as strongly as the bingers. These are the grumblers in life, always pessimistic, cynical, sarcastic. If the bingers are thunderstorms, maintenance rageaholics are endless rainy days.

By the way, some people do both. They are generally angry, like the maintenance ragers. And they have binges, too. These people have the greatest problems with anger. They only go from "angry" to "really angry" in their daily lives.

THE PATH TO FREEDOM: CALMNESS, MODERATION, AND CHOICES

"Okay, Ron and Pat, I admit it. I'm addicted to excitatory anger. I want that anger rush. Now what?"

You get to *crunch time* in each chapter of this book—the time to make a decision. Are you only going to learn about your anger, or are you going to do something about it?

It's crunch time right now, if you're addicted to excitatory anger.

How much do you need to change? Are you ready to take every needed step to become unaddicted? Are you willing to trade off the anger rush for something better? If so, read on.

Penelope and Paul are excitatory anger addicts. They've been walking on the same old path a long time. Finally they come to a crossroads. One sign points toward More Anger. The other points toward Freedom. They choose Freedom.

They have to go through three towns before they get to Freedom. The first is Calmness. Next is Moderation. And then comes Choices.

"Calmness, ugh!" Penelope hates calm. To her that means boring, depressed, wasted time. She can't figure out why anyone would want to be calm. But she plods through the town, with Paul's help. "Come on, Penelope. Learn to relax. You've been angry and upset for twenty years. Try something new."

Then it's Paul's turn to rebel. "Moderation!" he shouts, making it sound like a dirty word. Paul's an all-or-nothing guy. He thinks moderation means average, and he's never average. Penelope helps him, though. She reminds him that his all-or-nothing thinking is what sets off his rages. "You're a dead duck when anything goes wrong, Paul. You always turn little annoyances into a huge crisis. You'll never get better that way."

Finally, they get to Choices. What a place. Why, they haven't had choices in years. They had to get mad. Anger ruled their lives. When Anger said, "Raise a stink," their only question was, "How high?" Now they can actually choose whether they're going to get angry, how often, how much, and when to stop.

Paul and Penelope finally get to Freedom. They can stay there as long as they like, if they remember to stay calm, be moderate, and make choices.

Calmness

One day our friend and colleague Bruce Carruth asked, "What is the opposite of anger?" It took awhile to come up with *calm*.

Then we looked up "calm" in a few dictionaries. Some of the definitions include: still, without rough motion; a period of serenity; an undisturbed state; freedom from disturbance; and, specifically, to regain emotional control after anger (to calm down).

But here's the clincher. The word "calm" comes from old Greek (*kauma*) and Latin (*calere*) words that mean "burning heat" and "be hot," respectively. It's time to rest when things get too hot, inside or outside of you. Time to get calm.

Excitatory anger addicts are used to heat. Think of the ways to describe an angry person. Seeing red. Becoming livid. Boiling. Flaring up. Burning. Blazing. Fuming. Hot-blooded. Hot under the collar. Steamed. Inflamed. The heat of battle. That adrenaline surge literally warms them as their blood circulates faster. That's a big part of the anger rush.

The need for heat has got to go. It must be replaced with calmness.

Calm is the trade-off for the anger rush. That's because you can't be both calm and agitated at the same time. Calm means staying cool under pressure. Learning how to relax. It's an entirely different feeling than rage. Calm means staying in control of your mind and body instead of giving in to the anger addict's demand for action. It means staying sane at all times.

But how? After doing just the opposite for years, how do you learn to stay calm? It takes practice, lots of practice. It begins with a promise: *I promise to stay calm all day today.* Just one day. If it works, try another day. If you can't stay calm, find out why and do something about it.

To stay calm you have to relax. Relaxation is a skill you can learn. The more you relax, the better you get at it.

Ron made several suggestions to help people relax in his book *Angry All the Time*. We're repeating them here because they work.

Soften your eyes. You simply can't work yourself into a rage without an angry face. So don't glare, stare, or squint. Instead, let the small muscles around your eyes relax. Every time you begin getting upset, soften your eyes.

Breathe slowly and deeply. Take ten slow, deep breaths, counting them out loud. Feel the air going all the way down into your abdomen. Feel it go out. Don't think about anything else while you're taking those ten deep breaths.

Talk quietly. Keep your voice at its regular speed, loudness, and pitch. Remember that a lot of anger addicts think they only get loud when others hear them yelling. If you hear your voice changing, treat it like a wandering dog. Tell it to come back where it belongs, right now.

Tighten a few muscles and then relax them. Do this with the ones that seem the tightest. Include your shoulders, fists, jaw. This is a shortened version of a classic relaxation training technique that's been used for years.

Think relaxing thoughts. What good is a relaxed body without a calm mind? You need to tell yourself things like "I will let myself relax right now" or "I will stay in control. Just relax."

There are many good books on relaxation. We recommend you get one and read it often. One we suggest is *The Relaxation & Stress Reduction Workbook*, by Martha Davis, Elizabeth Robbins Eshelman, and Matthew McKay. Practice, practice, practice. Go to a relaxation training class or group if you need to. It's worth it. Eventually relaxing will become second nature to you, and you'll wonder how you did without it.

Moderation

Moderation means not going to extremes. It's the opposite of an all-or-none thinking pattern.

All-or-none thinking is the fuel that keeps the excitatory anger addict's fire raging: "She always treats me like dirt." "Those kids never do what they're told." "Nobody loves me." "I always get mad." All-or-none thinking makes a person rigid and brittle. Inflexible.

Little Annie comes home fifteen minutes late. She should get a warning, a reminder to come home on time. But that's not what her father does. This is a perfect excuse for him to rage. "How dare you come home late again! You never come home on time. You're always late. I'm really mad at you." The scariest part is that he believes it. His all-or-none style distorts his thoughts. He thinks he sees things as they are, but he's looking at life through a smudged window. He only sees black and white in a world full of colors.

All-or-none thinking supports all-or-none anger. The chronic alcoholic says, "I never have one or two drinks, Ron. When I drink, my goal is to get totally blitzed." The excitatory anger addict says, "Well, Pat, I never get a little angry. I always blow my stack."

There is one big difference between the alcoholic and the rageaholic, though. Total abstinence is the goal of the recovering alcoholic. Quitting completely. That's necessary because few alcoholics can ever learn to be social drinkers. Their bodies demand alcohol.

Excitatory anger addicts are more like compulsive overeaters. Compulsive overeaters can't set the goal of complete abstinence from food. They'd starve to death. Instead, they try to abstain from binge-eating episodes while learning to eat moderately.

Anger is a natural emotion. It's been part of being human since humans started being. You need some anger to survive. Anger signals that there's something seriously wrong that you should notice.

What's not needed, though, is the anger rush. That's what hooks the excitatory anger addict. There are many other ways—far better ways—to feel good.

Here's what the excitatory anger addict's recovery package includes:

- Quit getting high on anger.

- Learn to be a little angry from time to time.

- Don't lose control or make a scene.

Exercise: You can do this exercise right now. It will help you learn how to express your anger in moderation. It's called the Anger Thermometer.

Think of anger as if it were a thermometer. At the bottom of the thermometer are words like *annoyed, bothered,* and *upset.* In the middle are *mad, pissed off,* and *angry.* The top of the thermometer has words like *furious, fuming,* and *ballistic.*

The anger rush only kicks in at the top of the thermometer. To reach that "temperature," you need to get enraged. That's the part of the thermometer you need to avoid.

The left side of the thermometer has the words we just mentioned.

Ballistic   _____

Fuming   _____

Furious   _____

Angry   _____

Pissed off   _____

Mad   _____

Upset   _____

Bothered   _____

Annoyed   _____

The right side's for you. Make your own anger thermometer. Start at the bottom, putting in at least two words for mild anger. Then put in a couple for medium anger; then strong anger. Pick words that you actually use or will use.

Here are a few choices to help with the mild and medium sections. If you're an excitatory anger addict, you won't need help with strong anger.

dislike	ticked	bugged	provoked	displeased
grouchy	offended	miffed	sulky	piqued
rankled	riled	snarly	snappy	sore
irritated	vexed	disturbed	irked	troubled

Your personal thermometer needs at least five words, two for mild anger, two for medium, and one for strong. Keep this list in your pocket at all times. Use it to tell others exactly how angry you are. Even more important, get in the habit of using mild and moderate anger words while you practice staying calm. You can stay calm while you express your anger, but only at the mild and medium levels. *You can express your anger with no anger rush, but only at the mild and medium levels.*

Choices

Excitatory anger addicts are slaves. Their master is anger. But they can escape into freedom by remembering that they always have choices. They never have to get angry, no matter what others say or do.

The goal is freedom from psychological addiction. But you can't be free when the anger rush controls your life. Recovering alcoholics soon learn to say no. If not, they'll be drinking with their buddies that night. Compulsive overeaters have to say no to snacks, sugars, lots of stuff. Rageaholics must say no to the anger rush and no to a lot of chances to get angry.

We like the concept of anger invitations. An anger invitation is anything that happens that gives you an opportunity to get mad. The car that cuts in front of you. Your alarm clock going off. Cold coffee. Bossy parents. Your dog peeing on the rug. The trouble is that anger addicts (and others with serious anger problems) accept every invitation. They've never met an anger invitation they didn't like. Anger addicts go even one step further. They turn anger invitations into rage invitations so they can get high.

Most people probably receive several anger invitations a day. Anger addicts get many more, though. They go looking for them.

There's only one way to quit being a rageaholic, though. You must choose to decline almost all anger invitations.

"No, thank you. I think I'll pass. Yeah, I would've gotten really steamed about that before, but not today. I'm just not gonna let it bother me."

All your friends and family expect you to get angry a lot. They'll be amazed when you turn down their anger invitations. They may even send you a few extra ones just to check things out. So be prepared to say no to many anger invitations every day. They'll get the idea after a while, though. You're not the loudmouth you used to be. Your short fuse has been replaced with a longer one. You can live without the anger high. You're not a slave to your anger anymore. Saying no to anger rages means saying yes to calmness, moderation, and choices.

If you're addicted to excitatory anger, you've been accepting a lot of anger invitations. In fact, some days you're sure that people are doing things just to make you angry. Remember that you don't have to go to every anger party you're invited to. Also, remember these four phrases: Smart fish don't bite. Smart fish make their own decisions. Small fish get to be bigger by not biting on a lure just because it's there. Smart fish live a long time by not biting on anger lures. So when you think someone's going fishing for your anger, don't bite on that lure.

You can practice becoming a smart fish right now, by writing down a few things that you always get angry about. Decide on one or two to start with, and determine that when you see those lures, you'll remember those four phrases, and refuse to bite. When you practice this, you'll find that your attitude begins to change—and that other people begin to change their behavior, too. You aren't so busy reacting to them. And they aren't so busy reacting to you.

IV

Chronic Anger Styles

9

Habitual Hostility

Anger, anger, everywhere
It's time to raise a stink
Anger, anger, everywhere
There is no need to think

"Pat, I don't get it. Today I woke up at half past six. By seven I was in a fight with my wife. Then I got mad at my kids. Over nothing. It went on like that all day. And that's an average day for me. I'm angry all the time, but there's no real reason. I don't like this at all."

What a miserable life!

Sadly, that's exactly how thousands of people in this country live. They're angry all the time, and they don't even know why. Sure, they can always find something to get angry about. Anybody can. But most people discover that it's no fun being that angry. Most people learn to pick their fights carefully. They get angry when there's something seriously wrong. They ignore all those extra anger invitations to get mad about minor annoyances. They don't want to be angry too often because anger feels uncomfortable.

Habitually angry people continually repeat a pattern even though it brings bad results. Their anger causes problems again and again. Unlike the excitatory anger addict, they don't enjoy their anger or seek an anger rush. They know they should stop but don't.

HABITUAL HOSTILITY: LOOKING FOR THE WORST IN EVERYTHING—AND FINDING IT

The anger habit consists of two things: perpetually hostile ways of thinking and repeated, automatic actions. Here are the results. Habitually hostile people:

- *Expect the worst from people and life.* Most chronically angry people are pessimists. They are generally gloomy, depressed, unhappy individuals. Of course, good things do happen in their worlds occasionally, but they always expect bad things to follow. And when unfortunate events do occur, then chronically angry people expect even worse events to follow.

- *When in doubt, they always interpret events in a negative manner.* The official name for this pattern is the *hostile attributional bias.* That's a fancy way of saying that habitually angry people hear any positive remark as a neutral comment at best. For example, they hear "That's a nice shirt you're wearing" as "Well, it's barely acceptable but at least it's better than the one you wore yesterday." They hear neutral remarks as negative attacks. In their minds "I'll meet you at noon for lunch" becomes "I'll meet you at noon for lunch, but I'm telling you this because you are such a forgetful ignoramus." And they hear a relatively minor criticism as a devastating assault. So, "I don't like it when you swear" may be interpreted as "You hate me, don't you?" Their negative interpretations of other people's remarks often leave their partners, friends, and colleagues wondering, "Why in the world did he get so pissed off about what I just said?"

■ *They get angry about almost everything.* We often speak of "anger invitations" in our work with angry people. An anger invitation is anything you might get angry about *if* you accept that invitation. Here are some examples: someone cutting you off in traffic; cold coffee; your boss's suggestion that you come in a half hour earlier, and so forth. Although most people learn early in life that they should not accept too many anger invitations simply because getting mad causes so much hassle, habitually angry people have never met an anger invitation they didn't like. It's as if they are saying, "Sure, I'll get angry about that. Thank you very much."

■ *They look for more opportunities to practice their anger.* Habitually angry people don't just sit around waiting for anger invitations to drift their way. No, that's far too passive. Instead, they go looking for them. They think ahead, too; for instance, they can work themselves into a rage on the way home because they think that their kids haven't cleaned their rooms before checking the situation. They create arguments, too, because they expect conflict.

It would be a gross understatement to say that this way of living isn't pretty. It's really much worse than that. People who are habitually angry and hostile are some of the least contented individuals we've ever met. After all, who would want to live a life that is totally dominated by anger?

CAUSES OF HABITUAL HOSTILITY

How can this be? Everything is supposed to have a reason. Nothing just happens. So why do some people get and stay angry when it doesn't do them any good? The answer, we think, lies in each person's brain functions and personal history.

There is no single anger gene that causes people to be habitually hostile. However, everyone's brain is unique and some brains are constructed in ways that make their owners more likely to get angry than the average person. Furthermore, even apparently minor brain damage from falls, accidents, and beatings can impair a person's ability to control his or her angry thoughts and aggressive actions.

Damage or impairment of several areas of the brain have been found to be involved. These include the prefrontal cortex (our "executive control center"), the temporal lobes at the sides of the brain, and parts of the emotionally focused limbic system called the amygdala and hippocampus. There are specific medications that help some people become less angry and hostile, including antidepressants, antiseizure medications, and antipsychotics. But when should anyone with long-term anger problems (like the ones just described) explore taking these medicines?

Here is our suggestion. First try to change things without medication. See if you can break the habit of hostility and anger by reading books like this, making a firm commitment to change your behavior, talking with friends and counselors if need be, and so forth. Do everything you can to learn how to be less angry and more contented. But if that does not work after three to six months—if you still get angry just about each and every day, or you lose control of your anger, or you hurt others even once in a great while—then please make an appointment for a consultation with a therapist, psychologist, or doctor.

Now let's turn to personal history as a cause for habitual hostility.

As children, habitually angry people may have learned that anger worked. They got what they wanted with anger. Maybe they discovered that their parents gave in to tantrums. All they had to do was throw themselves on the floor and hold their breath until they turned purple, and they'd get that ice cream cone or a ride in the front seat or a day off from school. Perhaps getting angry was the only way to get attention in their families. Grumpiness may have worked, too. They would just mutter, grumble, and complain for a while and everybody came running.

The more they became angry, the better they got at it. They kept practicing, learning this skill. Finally, the behavior became automatic. They didn't have to practice anymore. They could, and did, get angry without thinking. They had developed the habit of anger.

There's another piece of history for habitually angry people. Many of them come from angry families. They saw Mom or Dad or both parents get mad a lot. They figured that what worked for Mom and Dad should work for them. They copied what they saw. Children don't question these things. They don't compare their parents with others until much later. They simply try to act like them. The reason to be angry was to be like their parents, not to solve real problems. Years later, they're still copying their folks, even though they know now that getting angry a lot is a mistake.

Other habitually angry people went through a long period of bad times. Illness. Poverty. Parental separation or divorce. Physical or sexual abuse. They gradually became bitter and hostile. Life gave them lemons, so they became sour. True, the bad times went away. Their illness cleared up. They aren't so poor anymore. Their parents got back together or went on with their lives. But somehow they never got over their anger.

We could spend hours trying to find out what good their anger is doing today. But that's not the point. They're not getting angry because of today. They're angry because of yesterday. They're angry because they're angry. Their anger habit keeps them stuck in old behavior.

THE GRUMP

Have you read A. A. Milne's *Winnie the Pooh?* It's a wonderful children's story about a bear named Winnie the Pooh, a tiger named Tigger, and several other characters. One very special animal is Eeyore, a dour donkey.

Eeyore is never happy. He's the resident pessimist in the book, always expecting things to go wrong. Nobody will remember his birthday, for example, but if they do he'll find ways not to enjoy the party. It's always going to rain on picnic days. Life goes from one problem to another. Eeyore is continually a little disappointed in a world that seems kind of gray and boring.

Eeyore is a grump. He's always muttering to himself. Nothing good is going to happen. If it does, it won't last.

Grumpiness is a form of habitual anger. It combines anger with sadness, like two rivers that merge to form a sea of misery. The grump often seems depressed, bitter, hopeless. Grumps believe that life will never be good. They don't realize that they are the ones creating their depression. They don't see that their own negative thoughts are what turn the clouds gray and bring rain to their picnics.

Grumps get irritated quickly. They're always a little angry anyhow, since they're looking for the worst in people. They don't necessarily fly into rages, though. Instead, they grouse around, complaining about little things: "Peter, I told you I wanted my bagel toasted and served with butter. You gave me jam! You never do it right." They make life uncomfortable for others, because nobody can please a grump.

Sometimes grumps develop rigid expectations that lead to disappointment. Mary expects Laurie to call her every two days. If Laurie only calls once in a week, Mary gets angry with her. She thinks Laurie doesn't care, and grumpily declares that she "can't count on her." But she didn't tell Laurie that this was what she expected. Even if she had, Laurie's calling once that week would not prove that Laurie didn't care about her. It might show that Laurie had a busy week. M. Scott Peck says, "Expectations are premeditated resentments." Pat says, "Expect a lot and you will be frequently disappointed. Accept a lot and you will be frequently delighted." A habit of expectations often leads to a habit of chronic anger.

THE ANGER HABIT IS AUTOMATIC, COMPULSIVE, AND FEELS NORMAL

"Hey, hon, what's the name of that great actor who plays the assistant district attorney? You know, the guy with glasses who's kind of short. He's the same one who played the villain in that other show, I think."

Habits are like character actors in the movies. They show up all the time, they're good at what they do, and no movie could get produced without them. But, somehow, you can never quite remember their names or describe them.

Habits have three important traits that help explain their power and invisibility. They are automatic, they feel normal, and they are compulsive.

Habits Are Automatic

Biting your fingernails. Brushing your teeth. Parting your hair on one side. Driving the car. Signing your name. All these, and so many more, are habits. You don't think about them. You just do them. It's not a habit if you have to think.

Habitual anger is just as automatic for some people. They don't think about getting mad. That's just what they do. For example, Mike, Melody, Tess, and Helen are having a great time playing the fantasy game. Then someone knocks on the door. Mike, who gets scared easily, worries that he's done something wrong. Melody, who loves people, shouts out a cheery welcome. Helen, anxious and overwhelmed, groans because she assumes the knock will mean more work for her.

Meanwhile, Tess is getting riled. She's thinking, "How dare anybody interrupt our game! I don't know who's out there, but they better have a damn good reason."

"Who is it?" she snarls, her anger obvious to everybody.

Mike has a habit of fear, Melody of joy, and Helen of worry. We'll write about them in another book. Tess is the one we're interested in now, because she's habitually angry.

Tess's angry response is immediate. She doesn't stop to think about it. That's typical for habitually angry people. Tess has been so angry so long that her thoughts, words, and actions are fixed. She got angry at that knock because she almost always gets angry when something unexpected happens.

If Tess were a computer, anger would be her default setting. A default setting is the one in control until someone changes it, just as a printer will continue turning out twenty-five lines to a page until the setting is changed. Tess has to consciously override that anger setting to feel anything else. She simply won't feel fear, or joy, or sadness, or anything else until she can learn how to turn off her anger.

Great idea, but how do you turn off anger? Compared to a computer, the brain is far more complicated. You can't simply flip a switch or write a new program. The anger habit has been built into your head, the product of thousands of repetitions. Also, every time you get angry, the anger habit gets a little bigger. Anger is a habit that feeds on itself and grows stronger in the process.

Automatic thinking and actions can be changed, though. The first step is to make your behavior fully conscious. We'll describe how to do that later in this chapter.

Habits Feel Normal

Habits aren't something you think about. They wouldn't be habits if you noticed them a lot.

Eating three meals a day is a habit for most Americans. Now, you might spend hours trying to decide what to eat for breakfast, lunch, or dinner. But you seldom ask yourself whether or not you want those meals. You don't even ask yourself if you're hungry. Seven o'clock in the morning means breakfast time. That's all there is to it. It feels normal to eat breakfast then, and not at two o'clock in the afternoon.

Anger has become normal for those with an anger habit. That seven o'clock fight has been patterned in almost as strongly as breakfast. In fact, they may go together. It's normal to fight at breakfast time. Pass the butter. Go to hell.

Habits are predictable. We always ask about habitual fights when we do couples counseling. These are the fights you can do in your sleep. First I say this, then she does that, then I do this, and she says that, and . . . These fights don't feel good. They cause pain even after the 500th time. But neither partner knows how to stop them. They are part of the routine. They are easy to start because all you have to do is say the trigger word or phrase. "Your mother . . ." "You are lazy." "Your weight . . ." "The house is messy." After that you're both on autopilot.

It's hard to stop a habitual fight.

Ron: Joe, Sally, you're doing it again. First Joe called Sally a liar, as usual. Then Sally defended herself and called Joe a bully. Now it's Joe's turn to tell Sally she's crazy, isn't it? Why don't you stop now instead?

Joe: But, Ron, she is crazy.

Sally: Oh, no I'm not. You're the one who's crazy, you stupid moron.

Ron: Whoa, slow down. Do you really have to keep doing this? Can't you stop?

Joe: Sure I could, Ron, but she is crazy. Not only that, she's heartless and selfish.

Sally: I am not. I'm the only one who cares about anyone, you self-centered oaf.

On and on it goes. This couple is paying good money to hire a counselor. Then they ignore him.

Habits insist on being played out completely. Joe and Sally are like someone who bites her nails and is only on the third finger. She has to finish that hand, no matter what the results.

Getting and staying angry feel absolutely normal to those with an anger habit. Peace is abnormal. So are calmness, negotiation, and letting go of anger.

Habits Are Compulsive

"Oh, sure, I can stop being angry. It's just a bad habit I picked up a few years ago. I'll just stop."

Don't bet on it.

People don't realize how powerful and demanding their habits are until they try to break one. The habit can be as small as putting on your right shoe first. It can be as serious as trying to quit drinking. The resistance is tremendous.

Worse, habits are like guerrilla fighters. They don't come out into the open very often. Most of their power is at the unconscious level. For instance, we've seen one alcoholic swear he'll never touch another drop. Meanwhile, his hand was opening the refrigerator and reaching for a beer. He truly did not know what he was doing, but he was doing it.

Anger is a demanding and controlling habit. If it could talk, this is what it would say: "Listen, pal. I'm in control. I'm doing all the thinking around here. You're gonna do things my way, or else." He means what he says, too. Just try to quit being angry for a while. You'll probably feel anxious. You won't know what to do or say. You'll have to think carefully about every step you take. Besides, that anger habit is sneaky. Put down your guard for a second, and suddenly you'll hear yourself yelling at someone. "How did that happen?" you'll ask yourself. "I thought I had my anger under control. Then, boom, I lost control."

To summarize, habitual anger:

- Was learned years ago, usually in childhood

- Is a product of thousands of repetitions

- Serves no particular purpose anymore

- Consists of hostile thoughts and negative behaviors

- Keeps people angry without good reason

- Happens without much thought or choice (is automatic)

- Feels perfectly normal to the person who is angry

- Powerfully resists change (is compulsive)

- Results in a person who gets mad too quickly and stays mad too long just because that is what he or she does

ENDING HABITUAL HOSTILITY

Habits are powerful. Taking them on head-to-head is difficult. But they have a fatal flaw. Habits are dumb as a post. You can sneak up on a habit if you know how.

Examine Your Angry Thoughts and Actions

The first step away from habitual anger is to become totally aware of how your anger works. Like a vampire, habitual anger mostly operates in the dark. Shining the bright light of knowledge upon it will go far to drive it away.

All behavior consists of actions, thoughts, and feelings. The trouble is that habits make your behavior mostly unconscious. Your job is to break through into full consciousness.

Let's start with your habitually angry actions. These are the things you do automatically that make your anger worse. First look at what you do with your body. Do you make your hands into fists? Speak loudly? Pace around? Grimace? Breathe quickly and shallowly? Now think about the words and actions that announce your anger to the world. Do you throw things? Constantly grumble? Complain for the sake of complaining? All these behaviors contribute to your anger. They tell your brain there is danger out there and you should prepare to fight.

Habitually angry people think negatively. Their overall worldview—the way they see the universe—is slanted toward problems, worries, and troubles. They assume that the world is a bad place full of awful things waiting to happen to them. This is the unconscious part—the assumption that the world is bad and dangerous. That's what has to be brought to full awareness and challenged.

It's easy to get angry with a mind full of negative thoughts. Without thinking, habitually angry people carry their anger with them, like a sack of rocks, just in case they need one. If they carry them long enough, they might even forget they are there.

The habit of anger is efficient. You simply get angry, or grumpy, all the time, without having to think. That's what has to change, now, to break the habit. Resolve to take nothing for granted any longer. Never say, "Of course I'm angry." Don't allow your anger to be automatic. Learn everything you can about how your anger builds. The idea is to slow down the process and to make it conscious. Only then will you have the choices of when and how to get angry.

Visualize a New You

The second step will catch your habit completely by surprise. You must visualize yourself looking at life in a brand new way. With peace. Calmness. Joy. Without anger. Without that grumpy "life's bad now and bound to get worse" mind-set.

We've created a generalized image to show you what we mean. You may need to alter it a little to fit your situation, but here's the basic form for your positive visualization. Please read it a couple times, maybe put it on tape in your own voice. Now close your eyes, take a few deep breaths, relax, and see yourself in this changed state.

Right now I am relaxed and peaceful. This is exactly how I want to be. I feel safe and comfortable. I feel at peace with myself and the world. My breathing is deep and quiet. My nerves are calm. All my anger has slipped away, and I enjoy this feeling of serenity. I am content.

Today, this moment, the world feels good to me. I have my own special place in it. I have my family, my friends. I enjoy being with them. I like them. I sense their goodness and their kindness, and they sense mine. I feel safe with them. I trust them.

I hear myself talking with others—quietly, calmly. I hear their laughter mingle with mine. I hear the sounds of people playing and enjoying life.

I see friendly faces. I see smiling people inviting me to join them.

I like being happy. I like being free from anger. I will let myself be just this way whenever I want. It's my life and my choice to be calm and peaceful. I choose to have hope and joy.

This is not a one-time visualization. You'll need to repeat it regularly, perhaps changing it from time to time to keep it fresh.

Nothing, not even your anger, can stop you from doing this. The anger habit will weaken each time you do this imaging.

Cultivate a Habit of Optimism

The third step in ending the anger habit is to develop a habit of optimism. Grumps need this step the most. They're the ones who always see the worst side of things. If you're a grump, you must realize that you're the one causing the problem, not the world. The world out there just "is." It's neither good nor bad. You're the one who makes your days cloudy or sunny.

Habitually angry people are habitual pessimists. That must change. Pessimism guarantees that the habitually angry person will find all kinds of reasons to get and stay mad.

Martin Seligman, a respected researcher, has done a thorough study of optimists and pessimists. He discovered that optimists have three main traits. First, they believe that good things will last and bad things won't (*persistence* is the name of this trait). Next, optimists believe that good things will spread a long way while bad things don't (*pervasiveness*). Finally, Seligman discovered that optimists take more responsibility than pessimists for the good things that happen (*personalization*). The optimist, for instance, thinks that the promotion she just received is going to last, will lead to more advancement, and is a result of her own effort. The pessimist might look at that same promotion as temporary, leading nowhere, and just a matter of luck.

Habitually angry pessimists are negative alchemists. They are masters at turning gold into lead. They take people's compliments and find something wrong in them. "Oh, sure, you say you love me, but that won't last. You'll throw me away just like my last lover." Then they get angry at a world they see as mean and nasty.

Exercise: Here's an exercise that will help you change the habit of negative thinking.

Take a piece of paper and turn it sideways. Make three equal columns on it and label them like this:

Positive Possibility   **Neutral Possibility**   **Negative Possibility**

Now start with a few clear examples from your life. For instance, your partner left a message saying she'd be late for supper. Your job is to write down three possible responses to that message, for example:

- *Positive:* That's thoughtful of her to call and let me know what's happening.

- *Neutral:* That's information for me. It's not good or bad.

- *Negative:* She's being rude and mean to me by not coming home on time.

Your boss asks you to work overtime.

- *Positive:* Good, I can use the extra money. Time and a half really helps.

- *Neutral:* Good and bad. More money, less time for other things.

- *Negative:* Why me? He's picking on me by asking me to work longer.

You must learn to fill in that positive column. Otherwise, you'll turn good things into neutral or bad things. You'll also see only what's bad around you, and that only makes you angrier.

You must get at least to neutral. Even better, though, is for you to jump into positive. That means choosing to respond from the positive column. Since your partner is being thoughtful by telling you, thank her. Tell her you appreciate her taking the time to call. While you're working overtime, if you choose to do that, think about how you'll put the extra money to good use.

Does this exercise look stupid, mushy, silly, or even idiotic to you? That may mean you're the one who needs to do it the most. It's your angry pessimist who is trying to stop you from changing. Don't let it.

Practice, Practice, Practice

We view positive imaging and learning to think less angrily as a daily discipline. You've got to begin each day with a new vision of yourself, of the people around you, and of the whole world. Otherwise the habit of anger will sneak back. It's like grafting a new, healthy branch on a sick tree. You'll get much better fruit eventually, but you'll have to give the tree extra care and attention for a while.

Expect to fail sometimes. Certainly you'll forget once in a while. You'll get angry without thinking. The habit of anger will sneak in and take over. But keep practicing. Think more positively and act calmly. You'll gradually gain control over the habit of anger. The graft will take hold. Your new tree will be rich and plentiful.

10

Paranoia
(Fear-based Anger)

Question: How safe is the world we live in?

The fear-based answer: The world is not at all safe. You have to be very careful. Don't trust anyone. People lie, cheat, and steal. They'll try to take your money. They'll seduce your boyfriend or girlfriend. They'll even attack you, so be prepared to defend yourself at any moment. Don't let down your guard.

Fear and anger are deeply intertwined emotions. Each is necessary for survival and both are quickly routed through one part of the brain called the *amygdala*, which is part of the brain's quick response center. Fear and anger both react to the possibility of danger with a lightning-fast, only partly conscious response. Of course there are differences, too. While a threatening situation triggers fear to send out a "let's get out of here fast" message, the anger message is "Hell, no, let's stay and fight." Fight or flight depends upon which of these emotions is stronger at the moment of choice.

But life is complicated and sometimes people react with a "fight *and* flight" reaction instead of "fight *or* flight." What happens is that people become defensively angry, ready to fight because they are scared. Think of a company of soldiers surrounded by the enemy, running desperately as they try to break through to safety but stopping every few seconds to turn and fire on the enemy.

Some people live in a world that feels to them a lot like being continually surrounded by enemy soldiers. But at least in war you can usually recognize the enemy. What if everybody you see looks and acts friendly at first but then turns on you? What if many of the people you most needed to trust when you were growing up turned out to be unreliable or even dangerous? The question then becomes "Well, then, whom can I trust?" and the unfortunate answer is "nobody." The result is people who perpetually stay on guard duty. They don't even trust their lovers, partners, and friends. They develop fear-based anger, a readiness to "fight back" against the attacks they think are always coming at them.

Distrust is the hallmark of people with fear-based anger. Their distrust of others makes them look for evidence that people are against them. Then their fear merges with their anger and they attack.

It's likely that everyone has felt fear-based anger from time to time. Imagine, for example, the woman who discovers her husband has been scrutinizing pornography on the Internet. She confronts him, he admits it and pledges to stop his behavior, but she remains doubtful, scared, and irritable with him for several weeks or even months. Her husband wants her to quit being so quick to accuse, and she wants to be done with it, but the combination of fear and anger just doesn't go away very quickly once it's been triggered.

Unfortunately, some people develop a pattern in which their fear-based anger becomes habitual. These people become excessively suspicious and distrustful of others. They think that others are trying to hurt them when there is no evidence that they are. Of course, we don't recommend that you blindly trust people. But most men and women are pretty good at deciding whom they can count on. They base their decisions on what the other person does. They trust those who earn their trust. They distrust those who are dishonest, irresponsible, dangerous, or distant.

The world of fear-based people is different. Nobody can be trusted, no matter how reliable they've been. It's difficult to earn their trust. Long ago, they decided that the world is full of enemies. Now they search constantly for proof that they are right. If they could use their suspiciousness as a dowsing rod, they'd find water every time.

We'll use the word *paranoia* to include all situations in which people become overly suspicious of others' motives and actions. But paranoia is also an anger style. That means paranoia can become a habitual way of dealing with the world.

Probably everyone has a little paranoia in them. That basic distrust helps protect people from being used and abused. And there certainly is some truth to the old joke, "just because you're paranoid doesn't mean they aren't out to get you." Paranoia, in small doses, helps you survive. Better a little suspicion now than a lot of regret later.

Some people have more than their fair ounce of suspicion, though. A few measure their distrust in pounds. They're the ones who are always "waiting for the other shoe to drop." They get along decently with others. But underneath their friendliness is a layer of doubt. They're never quite certain they can fully let down their guard. They'll tell you about past wounds that haven't completely healed. They want to trust, but . . .

Then there are those who measure their misgivings by the ton. They don't doubt, they *know* that nobody can be trusted. They are certain that others will betray, abandon, neglect, abuse, and harm them. The only question is when.

These two groups, the doubters and the total distrusters, have a paranoid anger style.

THE MASK OF INNOCENCE

The anger of people with strong paranoid tendencies sometimes comes out particularly sharp-edged, mean, and irrational. A woman named Marcy may scream, "I hate you, you're evil, you're just like your mother!" knowing very well that is the most hurtful accusation she could make against her partner, Billy. Furthermore, it's not Billy who has been acting like his mother lately—it's Marcy. So what is happening here? The answer is that Marcy, like many people with fear-based anger, frequently gives away to others her own angry thoughts. The technical name for this process is *projection.*

Projection occurs whenever someone gives away some unacceptable part of themselves such as their aggressive urges or their unacceptable sexual desires. One of the reasons, then, that Marcy is convinced Billy is out to hurt her is because she has projected her own desire to attack him. That way, as we will soon demonstrate, she can feel like an innocent victim who gets angry only because everyone else is so nasty.

Paranoid anger is both a chronic and a masked anger style. It is chronic because people become continually defensive, always both fearful and angry. It is masked because they confuse their own anger and aggression with others'. Their fearfulness and certainty that others cannot be trusted makes them think they are merely defending themselves against attack. What other people see, though, is a person who is attacking them for no reason. Instead, paranoids think others are always angry at them; they are just innocent victims.

Here's how you can put on the mask of paranoia. First, become convinced that someone is out to hurt you. Feel afraid but also become very, very angry that that person would want to harm you. Become so pissed that you'd like to hurt them. Think how pleasant it would be to smack them around, or destroy their possessions, or take away their lovers. Raw aggression!

But no, you can't do that. You're not supposed to get angry. That's not acceptable. You might get punished. No aggression allowed. Besides, you shouldn't be thinking those bad thoughts. Wipe them out of your brain! Quit fantasizing about hurting people. An aggressive thought is as bad as an attack. You'll be punished. You'll go to hell. You should feel very guilty whenever you get mad.

Now what? You're mad but you can't attack. You're upset but you can't have angry thoughts. You're too steamed up to bury your anger, like the avoider. And you're too excited to do nothing, like the anger sneak. Where's all that anger supposed to go?

Why not give it away? Play hot potato with your anger. Throw it out and let someone else catch it. Let them be angry at you, instead of you at them.

That's how paranoids put on their masks. They give away their anger to others. They *project* their anger outward. *Projection* means seeing characteristics such as anger in others, when they really belong to you. But they don't project their fear. Their fear makes them even more vigilant, distrustful, and ready to fight.

Paranoids see their own anger in the faces, words, and actions of others.

Here's an example. A few weeks ago Fred lost out on a promotion. Hank got the job instead. Is Fred angry? You bet he is. Does he see his anger? No. He thinks it's Hank who's furious with him. "Boy, is Hank ever angry. Why, he looks like he wants to tear me apart." Fred wants to clobber Hank, but he thinks it's the other way around.

Fred's fears often seem unrealistic, irrational. Hank doesn't look mad to anybody else. He looks perfectly normal. In fact, the paranoid has given his anger away. Fred doesn't recognize it, but he's actually looking in the mirror. Fred sees his own rage in Hank, and he believes Hank is dangerous.

Now comes an even more astonishing part. Fred, the paranoid, truly thinks he's threatened by Hank. He feels like an innocent victim. As far as Fred's concerned, he's done nothing to bother Hank. But if he doesn't do something fast, Hank could hurt him.

Fred figures he has the right to defend himself. And so he does. He marches over, tells Hank he knows what he's up to and he'd better stop it right now, or else! Fred thinks he's protecting himself, and in a way he is. He defends against the anger he sees in Hank. But that anger is actually his own. Fred ends up being able to justify his aggression this way.

Let's summarize the paranoid mask. Paranoids are unable to accept their desire to attack others. They project their anger, thinking others are mad at them. Then they protect themselves against the other's anger. They become defensive, suspicious, and hostile. But they don't feel guilty because they think they're only protecting themselves.

Paranoia is complicated. But it boils down to this: paranoids can only accept their anger when they feel innocently attacked by others. Then they can fight back without guilt.

GREED, GUILT, AND GUARD DUTY

"I want it all!"

Greedy people want everything in sight. They can be mean and angry, all right, like a hungry mutt growling and snarling, driving all the other dogs from a meal. Greedy people are never satisfied. They want more and more and more.

Greed. Wanting too much. Pigging out. Grabbing more than your share. Greed is not exactly a nice feeling. Unchecked, it can destroy the trust we have in others. Who wants to believe that everyone else is just waiting for a chance to pounce, to steal what is yours?

Most people are secretly greedy. But they learn to control their impulses. They quickly realize that others will fight back if they get too demanding. The only way to relax is to share the goodies. Sometimes greed sneaks out, though, such as when a wealthy parent dies and the children fight over the legacy.

Guilt is another reason people limit their greed. People feel guilty when they want too much, especially if that means wanting to take things that belong to others. Paranoid people constantly fight off the guilt associated with greed. In order not to feel guilty, they try to give all their greediness away to others, just as they do with their anger.

People with a paranoid anger style are sure that others want to take whatever is important to them. Their belongings, their jobs, their partners, their children, their lives—none of these are safe. They're never greedy themselves, naturally. It's those others who can't be trusted.

Paranoids are constantly on guard duty, like soldiers under siege. They never take breaks. They never relax. Instead, they scrutinize the people around them, always ready to challenge. "Halt, who goes there?" They're looking hard to find any suggestions of greed, anger, danger. They suspect everyone. And they're awfully good at finding evidence, even if others don't agree. "See that nasty look! The sort of scowl she just made. What do you mean, you don't see anything. I'm sure she's angry at me. She must be mad because I bought that new car."

It's bad enough that paranoids see greed where there isn't any. It's tragic that they think others are out to get them. But these guards are dangerous. They shoot down all their enemies, claiming self-defense. They see themselves as victims, not attackers. They attack the other's motives, goals, personality and try to get everybody to sympathize with them. Sometimes they succeed, and then everyone attacks the other person. More often, people begin to avoid the paranoid. Who wants to hang around someone who is convinced the whole world is plotting against them?

A Practical Exercise

A big problem for you if you have a paranoid anger style is reacting to others with rage before you realize what you are doing. Giving your feelings of anger away and keeping the fear is a good mask—so good that sometimes you won't even know you are wearing it! You may go off half-cocked to prove "they can't do this to me." But you are only shooting yourself in the foot. Your impulsiveness and a tendency to defend yourself with angry actions that may not fit the real situation destroy your credibility. Other people stop trusting you, really do get mad at you, and think of you as dangerous and unpredictable.

Here is something practical you can do to control the damage your paranoid anger can cause. Find a small box, like a matchbox, and put a picture of a bare foot in it—or a foot wearing shoes just like yours. Keep it in your pocket. Every time you catch yourself thinking "they're really out to get me" (or your own favorite version of that thought), pull the box out of your pocket. Open it and look inside. Realize that you may be about to "shoot yourself in the foot" if you take any sudden action on that thought. In fact, you need to stop thinking that way. Take a few minutes to calm down, and get more centered again.

JEALOUSY AND ENVY: SPECIAL KINDS OF PARANOIA

Envy and jealousy are complicated feelings. Anger is usually a major ingredient, but with it comes tinges of fear, sadness, shame, and other feelings. Here we'll concentrate on how envy and jealousy connect with anger and paranoia.

Envy: May Your Milk Turn Sour

Envy is the misery people feel when somebody else has something they want. It can be anything desirable, such as jewelry, fame, money, or someone's love or respect.

People who envy want what isn't theirs. If they can't have it, they hope the other person will suffer or lose what they have. True, the young woman agrees, it's awful that her neighbor has a bottle of sweet milk and she has none. "Oh, well," she says, "I'll just pray that the bottle of milk turns sour."

Envy is one reason people love to hear about the troubles of famous athletes, politicians, and actors. Oh, the joy of seeing these shooting stars plunge to the ground. If you can't have what they've got, at least you can root for their rapid demise.

Envy brings out a special kind of anger and meanness. It makes people want to attack and destroy what's good in others. Envious people see others' success as a sign of their own failure.

Paranoid people often believe that everybody envies them. What's really happening? It's those who are paranoid who are envious. They want to attack, destroy, and steal. Instead, they accuse others of wanting to do those things to them.

Exercise: Envy often comes out in many little acts of meanness. Here are some examples of angry, envious behavior: putting someone down behind their back; making fun of someone to make them lose confidence; criticizing something good that someone else has; insulting someone whose traits you envy—for example, calling someone generous "dumb" or a good money manager "cheap"; telling yourself you deserve what someone else has; giving someone who hasn't hurt you the cold shoulder because you envy them; giving someone you envy bad advice so they will look worse than you; stealing something from someone you envy (whether it is a material object or an attitude of joy or happiness).

Write down the envious actions in the previous paragraph that you have used against someone, without making any excuses about why it was okay to do them. These behaviors aren't okay. Ask yourself how you learned them, and what it is you really want in life. Work on changing these behaviors, one at a time, to behaviors that will help you get what you want with respect for yourself and for others.

Jealousy, Insecurity, Possessiveness, and Paranoia

Probably the best time to see how fear and anger interact to produce a "fight and flight" reaction is when people become jealous. That's when they become convinced that someone is trying to steal away their partner and/or that their partner wants to cheat on them. They become simultaneously terrified and furious. Jealousy makes people say and do stupid things, up to killing both their partner and themselves.

Here's how jealousy works. You feel jealous when you think another wants to take away something that belongs to you. We'll concentrate on sexual jealousy here, but you can jealously guard just about anything: water rights, a parking space, money, or a work responsibility. The main idea, in each case, is that you believe somebody wants what you have. Sometimes you're right, of course. But when jealousy develops into an anger style, you become paranoid—you see rivals everywhere.

Sexual jealousy is not so much an expression of love as of insecurity and possessiveness. People with this style of paranoia constantly feel that rivals are trying to steal their partner's body or love. They try to protect both their sexual rights and the relationship itself.

Take Sue, for instance. She gets nervous when Ted even looks at other women. And when he talks with them, one-to-one, she goes nuts. She demands to know why he does it. She accuses him of wanting to have sex with them. She demands reassurance, but just gets angrier when Ted tries. "Oh, sure, you say you're faithful," she wails, "but I don't believe you."

Sue is desperate. She tries to control Ted's actions, even his thoughts, because she's scared. She confuses love with ownership. She clings to Ted as if he were a life raft on the ocean. The tighter she grabs, though, the more she's afraid he'll slip away.

Not all jealousy is bad. A little is normal. It tells each partner that the other is important. It's normal to watch over and guard your treasures. Jealousy can also be a signal that something is wrong in the relationship. Maybe Ted isn't having an affair but he's been too wrapped up in work to notice Sue. Jealousy is a warning bell ringing danger, but sometimes that bell rings and rings for no reason. Then the jealousy causes trouble.

Too much jealousy destroys relationships. It takes the place of real intimacy. After a while almost every conversation leads back to the same routine: "Where were you, what were you doing, and with whom?"

Jealousy is also dangerous. The jealous person feels a strong sense of betrayal and desperation. People who would otherwise never harm anyone will shoot their unfaithful mate.

Extreme sexual jealousy, sometimes called irrational or insane jealousy, looks like this:

- *It goes on forever.* No amount of explanation or reassurance works.

- *It is intense.* You get more emotional, more upset than a situation merits.

- *It is obsessive.* You can't think of anything else. You are consumed by jealousy. All you do is worry.

- *It is paranoid.* Suspicions, accusations, mistrust haunt you. You search through his pockets for "proof" of an affair, you follow her "just to see where she's going," you listen in on phone calls. There must be something going on, there must be.

Remember also that paranoids give away "bad" feelings and desires, such as anger and greed. Why not sexual desire as well? Very jealous people often hide their own sexual impulses from themselves. They don't want to admit they've got their eyes and minds on someone else's mate. Too much guilt. So they think everyone else is boiling over with lust for others. All of them, whoever they are, want to seduce. But not them; the jealous person is innocent. "I have no evil sexual thoughts," says the very jealous person. "It's you, and you, and you . . ."

Exercise: Here's a memory device to help you with the warning signs of jealousy. Look at each letter and see how closely each characteristic fits you.

J = Judgmental

E = Eagle-eyed

A = Angry

L = Lonely

O = Oversensitive

U = Unforgiving

S = Scared

Write the letters and words on a note card and put it in your pocket. It can help you recognize the signs of a jealous attack early enough to find something healthier to do than have a fit. Use it to help yourself stay in control of your jealousy, and use it until you have successfully stopped an attack of jealousy several times in a row.

THREE WAYS TO BE LESS SUSPICIOUS

Fear-based anger is a mixed-up way of thinking. To change, you'll have to learn to think differently. That means learning to be less suspicious. You'll have to practice changing your thoughts. Otherwise, you'll quickly slip back into old habits.

Basically, you'll need to do three things. First, start recognizing and accepting your own anger. No more innocent victim games. Next comes dealing with your greed, envy, and jealousy. Third, you'll need to start trusting others more, which means challenging some very old ways of thinking about the world.

Recognize and Accept Your Anger

If you're paranoid and want to change, you must begin with this commitment: every time I think someone is angry at me I will assume it is me who is really angry at them.

Granted, some of the time they may be mad at you, too. But that's not your problem. It's their job to tell you that directly. If they're mad and say nothing, tough.

You've been giving away your anger. Now it's time to reclaim it. You must realize you're angry, a lot. Sometimes you want to hurt others, even to destroy them. You think nasty thoughts, just as many other people do.

Acceptance. Yes, I'm human. Yes, I get pissed. Yes, I'm an aggressor. Yes, I hate and lust and rage. Yes, I'm angry.

Expect a ton of guilt. You've been hiding your anger to avoid your guilt. But remember this: just because you think a nasty thought doesn't mean you're hurting anybody. Thoughts aren't actions. You're more likely to hurt others when you deny your anger than when you admit it to yourself. You have to accept your angry thoughts so you won't turn them into paranoia.

We suggest you keep a paranoia notebook. Write down who you think is pissed at you, and why. That's enough about others, though. Immediately ask yourself what you're angry at them about.

Here's a sample. "Henry's angry at me. I see it in his eyes. He must be mad because I'm better looking." That's your paranoid thought process in action.

Don't stop here, though. You've got to challenge the way you think and do things.

"No, that's not it. *I'm the angry one.* I've been bothered for months because Henry's been dating Joan. I want Joan and he's got her. I hate the way women hang around his office."

Never end a notebook entry until you have confronted your paranoia. That's the only way you'll be able to change how you think.

Deal with Your Greed, Envy, and Jealousy

You are certain that others want too much, that they want to destroy what belongs to you, and that they won't share what they have. You think others are greedy, envious, and jealous.

There's a whisper of truth in these ideas. Certainly *some* people are greedy, *some* of the time. Others are *sometimes* full of envy and jealousy. And, if you're paranoid, you've probably gotten very good at spotting those situations. Occasional moments of greed, envy, and jealousy are all part of being human—maybe not the best part, but undeniable nevertheless. The problem with paranoia is that you greatly exaggerate others' amount of greed, envy, and jealousy. That's because you're giving your own feelings away again.

We're right back to facing the truth. You've got to see yourself as you are: a sometimes greedy, envious, jealous, and even lusting human being.

Maybe you're worried that you'll be a sinner by facing this truth. But recognizing and accepting your angry and greedy thoughts doesn't make you a sinner. The thoughts have been there all along, remember. You just tried to give them to others because you could not accept them. Now you need to separate your urges, legitimate or not, from the urges of others. That can help you be more honest, fair, and good.

Every time you think others are greedy, envious, or jealous, ask yourself these questions: What do I want too much of? What do I want to destroy that belongs to somebody else? What do I want to take that belongs to others?

Think about these ideas carefully. You can keep these thoughts in your head, or you may want to write them in your paranoia notebook. This is your private journal, so be totally honest in it. Include your sexual desires, the ones you give away. For instance, you may think your partner wants to play around. There's no evidence, though. So who is it that *you* want to have an affair with?

Everything you think people want to do to you is what you want to do to them. Face that reality and you can get better. Deny it and you'll stay miserable.

Learn to Trust

We began this chapter by describing how paranoids distrust just about everybody. But now it's clear what that's all about. They distrust so much because they've given away all their anger, greed, and lust. In addition, they are terribly afraid that others want to attack them. "I'm innocent and vulnerable," says the paranoid. "You're mean and nasty and you want to hurt me."

Well, that's wrong. Others are not out to get you. They've got lots better things to do with their lives than spending all day thinking up ways to ruin yours.

You can learn to trust more. Of course, you must give up playing the injured victim. And you must accept your anger as yours, not theirs.

Most people decide on the evidence whether or not to trust. They usually believe in someone until he or she does something wrong. If someone screws them over, they fight back or get away fast. That's all we ask. Let the evidence decide the issue.

However, even fact-finding may be a problem if you are paranoid. You may not be a good judge of the evidence. You may be too eager to prove others are bad. You'll only search for negative hints and clues. You'll ignore good things. You've become awfully good at looking through the whole crate to find one bad apple. Then you claim that the whole bushel is rotten.

So here's our suggestion. Find at least two people who aren't paranoid. Ask them to help you learn how to trust others. When you start getting suspicious, defensive, or jealous, call them up immediately, before you become absolutely certain you're being victimized again. Tell them what you think you saw or heard. Have them carefully review your "evidence," which will often turn out to be vague. Have them ask you if there are any other explanations for what you think you've seen or heard. Maybe they can help you see things in a different light. And don't forget to check out your own anger and aggression.

Their job isn't to talk you out of your paranoia. They can only help you see things in more than one way.

Then it's up to you. You can stay convinced there's a plot. Who knows? Maybe this time you're right. But remember this: You're the one with a problem. You're the one who is paranoid. Unless there is absolute proof someone is out to hurt you, you'll do best to drop the accusation.

Eventually you won't need your friends' help. But you do now, because you have a distorted view of the universe.

Here are a few sayings that can help you trust more:

- Nobody spends all their time thinking up ways to hurt me.

- I can *choose* to trust.

- Give people the benefit of the doubt.

- Today I won't give away any of my feelings.

- I accept my anger, greed, and sexual desire as part of me.

- I don't have to defend myself because nobody is attacking me.

You have to live these sayings, not just mouth them. Try this: Put these six sayings (and you may want to add more) on separate slips of paper. Put them in a bowl. Each morning draw one slip from the bowl. Think about it. Use it all day. At night ask yourself how you did. Be sure to put the slip back in the bowl. You might draw it again the next day.

CREATE A SENSE OF SAFETY IN YOUR WORLD

People with fear-based anger run scared through life. Sometimes that's because the world they live in really is unsafe. If you live with someone who regularly threatens or attacks you, for example, your world is unsafe. The best thing you can do for yourself may be to get away from the danger.

However, people with paranoid tendencies tend to exaggerate the dangers in their world. They falsely feel endangered when nobody is attacking. Perhaps, if you see a lot of yourself in this chapter, it is time for you to get serious about changing your way of looking at the world. The brief sayings noted above can certainly help if you use them frequently, but perhaps you need more help than that. If so, please consider talking with a therapist who can help you challenge your fear-based irrational beliefs. Also, some people benefit from a class of medications called "antipsychotics" that can help them sort out real from imagined threats.

11

Moral Anger

What would you die for? Would you sacrifice yourself to save your children from a fire? To save a neighbor's child? Would you die for a cause, such as defending democracy or your religious beliefs?

What would you be willing to lose a job over? Would you blow the whistle on cheap building practices that harmed the general public? Would you risk losing your job by confronting your boss who was sexually harassing you? Would you resign to protest unethical hiring or firing practices that didn't directly affect you?

What would you fight for? Would you get into politics to campaign for a certain party or platform? Get into a fistfight to defend your honor? Would you ever risk a jail sentence by taking part in a street protest? If so, over what?

These are examples of moral anger, the anger people feel when their values or beliefs are threatened.

Moral anger goes by other names. One of them is outrage, another is righteous indignation. Outrage occurs when someone commits a horrible act, such as killing a child. People feel shocked, alarmed, and furious with the offender. Righteous indignation occurs in response to injustice. People fight for truth, justice, and fairness, at least as they see it. Those with much moral anger are often called judgmental.

Moral anger has great value. Here's an example.

Ron once worked at a stroke rehabilitation center. Every week the staff met to decide who to keep, who to discharge, and who to send to nursing homes for custodial care because they were not improving and the bed was needed for someone with a better chance of recovering.

Carlotta Smith seemed to be heading for the nursing home. She'd been on the unit a week. She didn't respond much to the doctor or therapists. She was a nice lady and her family loved her. But the unit needed that bed badly.

That's when Ellen Jensen, Carlotta's speech therapist, got mad. "How can you do this to her? She's only been here a week. We've got to give her more time!" Ellen shook as she spoke. She didn't usually do things like this. She wasn't a crusader. But she felt she had to take a stand here, even if others disagreed.

Ellen got her point across strongly. The doctor relented, giving Mrs. Smith another week. Sure enough, the next day, Carlotta began to squeeze her daughter's hand. By the end of the week she was able to say a few words. Carlotta left the unit three months later, discharged to her daughter's home.

This is one tiny example of the power of moral anger. On a larger scale, it can trigger social change, religious movements, and political upheavals. The American Revolution was fueled by righteous indignation ("Don't Tread on Me"); so was the Civil War, on both sides, which may explain why it was so deadly. At its best, people use their moral anger to fight for just causes. They may risk their lives, careers, and safety to defend their beliefs. If they die, they die with honor.

Too much moral anger, however, is dangerous. And it can become a habit, a style of living.

THE MANY SIDES OF MORAL ANGER

Certainly more people have died as a result of moral anger than all the other kinds of anger combined. An outraged husband attacks his unfaithful wife. The Hatfields and McCoys shoot each other to avenge the death of the last person killed in the feud. People find ways to justify millions of deaths, from the Crusades to World War II (largely a product of a madman's moral vision). More recently hundreds of thousands have died in the African country of Rwanda, and the anger continues in Israel, Northern Ireland, and Iraq.

Moral anger is dangerous because it combines anger with moral certainty. The morally angry person thinks, "I am mad at you. I am better than you. Therefore, I can attack and destroy you."

When you wrap yourself in the warm robe of moral superiority, you think everything you do is morally correct. You start to think that God is on your side. You think you are good, pure, holy, and proud. Others are bad, evil, sinful, and despicable. That's how you rationalize attacking them, even destroying them. You hurt others but feel totally justified. You attack others without guilt because they are bad.

Most people instinctively sense moral anger's danger. They try on that righteous robe with great caution. They sense that putting it on is a whole lot easier than taking it off. Most often they just want to live and let live. They reserve their moral anger for very serious occasions.

Some people get stuck in moral anger. They love to wear the robe of righteousness. It seems to fit so well they won't let it go. They like the color, the feeling, the style. They think moral anger is very becoming, and so they constantly become morally angry. They think of themselves as morally superior. A few truly believe they have a special contract with God. Their job, as they see it, is to crusade for justice. They often come across to others as sanctimonious, making a show of their holiness.

Others are more subtle but just as stuck. They're often heard saying things like this: "How could you even think that?" "How dare you question my authority?" and "I pity you." They seem to hold others in contempt, as if only they know the right path. They look down on others, dismissing their arguments as unworthy. The message they send is that they are simply better than others.

When moral anger becomes a life stance, it is a serious problem. People with this anger style look for things to get angry about. Then, when they find something, they demand that others obey in the name of justice. Morally angry people don't try to convince others with facts. Rather, they expect others to realize how righteous they are. "Obey me because I hear the word of God" too easily becomes "Obey me because I am the word of God."

Tactics of Moral Anger

Moral anger has two main parts. First comes an attitude of moral superiority, expressed as, "I'm better than anybody else, I know exactly what's right and wrong, I'm always on the good side." People with moral superiority believe their values are *truths*, and all other values are *lies*. They are smugly confident that they are better than others.

Some morally superior people are very subtle. They don't boast of their greatness. Instead, they tell others how disappointed they are in them. They hint that others aren't quite good enough. They raise an eyebrow instead of shaking their fist. But the message is the same: "I know the truth. My beliefs are the right ones. You are not as good a person as I."

The second part of moral anger is fighting with moral weapons. People with this anger style use their values like clubs. They beat others down with them.

"You're a slob, that's all. I'm the one who keeps things neat around here. If it weren't for me, you'd live in a pigsty."

"I'm rational and you're crazy. That's why the kids should listen to me."

"I'm an artist and you're just a plodder. I feel sorry for you."

"You're fat, ugly, and stupid. So shut up and do what I say."

Notice the contempt, the nose in the air. The message is "I am better than you." The weapon is moral anger.

Morally angry people are quick to act ethically superior in a fight. They use their morality as a tactic. The goal is to make others feel inferior. It's a way to win battles and get people to do what they want.

THE "STAND ON THIS CHAIR" TEST FOR MORAL SUPERIORITY

About now you may be wondering if you have a problem with moral superiority and moral anger. Here's one way to find out. You'll need another person to do this exercise with you, so ask a friend or family member for help. You'll also need two chairs.

Begin by sitting facing each other, just getting comfortable. Talk about anything noncontroversial, like the weather.

Now stand on your chair and have your partner sit on the floor. Look down on that person and tell him or her how you feel up there.

You might feel great. "Hey, I like it up here. I feel in control, power-ful," or "I feel really natural up here. I belong on the top of this mountain." Or you might not like it at all. "This is gross. I hate it. I feel out of place, shaky." Be honest with your feelings, though. You might feel that you really like it up there, but that would be bad and immoral, so you can't (at least you can't let anyone know). Be honest and don't edit. Don't say what you think you should say. Report exactly what you feel. Then have your partner talk about what it's like on the floor looking up at you.

You'll get off that chair in a minute or two. But first try this. Look down on your partner and say these phrases:

- I'm better than you.

- I know what's right better than you.

- I have better values than you.

- I'm right and you're wrong.

How true do those statements feel? How familiar? Are any of them old friends? Are they complete strangers, or a little of both?

Now reverse places. You sit on the floor and have your partner stand on the chair. Again, share your feelings and observations. Be sure to talk about yourself, not the other person.

Next step: Return to sitting on the chairs. Discuss what you have done. Get the feeling of both being equal.

All three positions have value. It's useful, for example, to get in touch with your desire to be powerful, dominant, superior. That's what standing on the chair is about. But there are times when sitting on the floor is good, such as when you want to learn something from a good teacher. And, of course, sitting together at the same level is important for sharing, teamwork, and cooperative abilities.

Ask yourself these questions: How comfortable am I in each posi-tion? Is one more attractive than the others? Am I afraid of any of the three places? Your answers will help you know where you need to grow.

You could have a problem with moral superiority if standing on that chair felt awfully familiar.

Now imagine yourself getting angry with someone. Do you automati-cally climb on top of the chair? Do you tell them they're bad because of their beliefs? Do you insist that you are right? Do you feel outraged because they dare to disagree with you? If so, then you argue from a stance of moral superiority. You have a problem with moral anger.

It's not wise to stand on top of that chair too often. Yes, there are times to take a stand. But beware of taking moral stands about nonmoral issues. There's no need to turn simple disagreements into moral warfare. It's like saying that the color red is better than the color yellow. Certainly you might prefer red to yellow. But they are only colors.

Joe wants to go to a movie and Merrill wants live theater. They have different preferences. Joe has no reason to tell Merrill that only selfish snobs go to the theater. Merrill has no cause to tell Joe that only dumb clods don't like theater. Each turns a simple difference into a moral battle. Each claims to be better than the other. Joe and Merrill are fighting over who gets to stand on the chair. They're both morally angry. Chances are they'll end up going nowhere, because they've quit discussing real differences.

So, how often do you climb onto that chair of moral superiority? How frequently do you get stuck there, feeling righteous, angry, and too proud to get off? Would you like a little help getting down?

CLIMBING DOWN FROM THE CHAIR

For the moment, we're going to turn that chair into a ladder, to show you the four steps in letting go of moral anger:

- Be humble (humility)

- Be understanding (empathy)

- Be flexible (flexibility)

- Be selective (selectivity)

Humility

We first described the principle of humility in our book *Letting Go of Shame*. The principle of humility states that all human beings are equal—nobody is better or worse than another.

Being humble means having respect for the inner dignity of every person. The Society of Friends (Quakers) says it well: "There is that part of God in everyone." But you've got to take a step down the ladder to see God in everyone. You've got to give up the attitude of superiority that fuels moral anger. That means giving up your claim to being morally better than others. People who think of themselves as morally superior are only demonstrating arrogance. The idea is to get off the ladder, not climb higher.

Humility means making a conscious decision to accept yourself as equal to others, neither better nor worse. But it's not enough to be humble most of the time, except when you're angry. Anger is no excuse to suddenly act superior.

There's no question it's hard to stay humble when you're angry. Who wouldn't want to strengthen their argument with the strong wine of moral righteousness? But remember that most disagreements are about preferences, not moral principles.

Here's a challenge. Every time you start to get mad, stop. Take a few seconds to look for part of God in the other person (or, if you wish, just look for the goodness in that other person). Search it out. Then speak to that part of them, to their beauty and goodness instead of their ugliness and badness.

You, too, have plenty of beauty. You are rich in the spirit that makes you equal with any other. Perhaps you need to search for that spirit in yourself as much as in them. Chances are that's not the part that wants to climb the ladder of moral superiority.

You may still be angry with the other person. There may still be big differences in how you see the world and what you want. But now you can approach the other as an equal, both standing on the same ground. Firm footing makes for fair fighting, based on mutual respect.

Empathy

Empathy means entering into another person's world. It means being genuinely interested in what they say, do, and think. Empathic people are willing to see the world through the eyes of others, even people very different from themselves.

Morally angry people have trouble with empathy. They are too certain they know exactly what is right (their way) and wrong (any other way). They're not curious about the reasons for the other person's behavior. Instead, they condemn without thinking.

Here's an illustration. Michelle and Bob are partners. One day Michelle tells Bob she has signed up for a class in computer technology. Bob hits the roof. "You don't need that class. It's a waste of money. Besides, you ought to stay home with the kids more. You're not a good mother because you're so selfish." Bob is using every moral argument he can think of. Michelle is careless with money. She's selfish. She's a bad mother.

Not once does Bob stop to ask Michelle why she's taking the class. If he did, she would tell him that she feels brain-dead doing nothing but watching the kids. She would mention that she can use what she learns to stimulate the children's minds.

Bob's not interested in that information, though. He's too busy criticizing Michelle. He thinks he knows exactly what's right and wrong.

Moral anger is as much about power and control as any other type of anger. Bob wants Michelle to feel guilty. Guilt is the favorite weapon of morally angry people. Bob hopes Michelle will feel so bad about what she's doing, and about herself, that she will do what he wants. Those with excessive moral anger must give up making others feel guilty.

Empathic people are curious. They want to know what others care about. They listen without condemning. They don't try to get everyone to think like they do. Instead, they appreciate the range of ideas and values that people have.

The best empathy exercise is listening—active, careful listening. Ask others why they do things the way they do. "Joe, what do you like about car racing?" (not "Car racing. What a waste of time"). "Helen, why did you choose to bottle feed?" (not "You shouldn't do that. It's bad for the baby"). "Marcus, why did you decide to become a vegetarian?" "Marlys, why did you switch from social work to accounting?"

Listen. Ask nonjudging questions. Listen more. Ask another question. Stop yourself every time you feel the desire to criticize. Don't let yourself climb on that chair again.

Flexibility

When Ron was a teenager, his father Miles married a woman who had disowned her son Ralph. Ralph had married outside their religion. Mother and son hadn't spoken or seen each other for five years. She felt awful about it but she wouldn't budge. Finally Miles asked her a question. "Minnie," he said, "do you really want never to see Ralph again, for the rest of your life?" The answer was no. That year Ron's dad arranged a reconciliation. Minnie still wished Ralph had married differently, of course, but now she had her son back.

Why was this so hard? How did Minnie lose her son for so long? The answer is that she had taken a rigid moral stance. She could not compromise or negotiate. She thought she had no options. She was stuck.

Morally angry people are expert at painting themselves into a corner. That's because they think too rigidly. Their view is right. The other is wrong. There can be no compromise.

People can become morally rigid about things far less serious than religion. For instance, Wilma wants to have Thanksgiving dinner with the entire family at her house, just as they do every year. But her son Tom's wife just had a baby. Tom and Ellie don't want to take the baby 100 miles to Wilma's. Instead, they suggest the family have dinner with them.

"That's not right," shouts Wilma. "We always have holidays at my house. I'm the mother and Thanksgiving should be at the parents' home."

Notice the word *should*. Morally angry people often use that word. You *should* do this. You *shouldn't* do that. *Should* implies a moral obligation. If you disobey a *should*, you *should* feel guilty and bad. When people use this word it is a good sign that they are using moral anger to get what they want.

Wilma won't budge. She's right, period. They're wrong. If they won't come to her house, there won't be a family gathering this year. Wilma is inflexible. She can't or won't adapt to new situations. Wilma doesn't modify her plans or actions to fit current reality.

People with too much moral anger need to gain some flexibility. The world keeps changing, after all, whether or not you want it to change. This key phrase is helpful: I believe this, but I'm willing to negotiate or compromise. Wilma, for instance, believes that Thanksgiving should be at the parents' house. Still, she could at least talk with Tom and Ellie. Maybe this year she could go to their home, and next year return to hers.

If you find that you are inflexible with others, you are probably that way with yourself, too. Most people who judge others harshly judge themselves harshly as well. Try this:

1. Make a list of all the things you think you should do.

2. Now, all the way down the list, change that word *should* to *could*.

3. Read your list from start to finish in two ways. First say, "I should do the floor today" or, "I should make that telephone call today." Then say, "I could do the floor today"

and, "I could make that telephone call today." Notice the difference in how those two sentences feel. Let yourself listen to the *could*, and make a choice about whether you want to do that particular thing today or not.

4.   Now make a list of things you think other people should do. Turn that list into a *could do* list, too. And for today, leave the choice to the other folks. It's really their choice anyway.

Morally angry people think that if they believe in something, they cannot compromise. That may be true once in a while. People do have to take a stand from time to time. But it's important not to get locked into rigid stances. Negotiation and compromise are part of life. Being flexible and not so judgmental with yourself and others will improve your self-esteem and your relationships. You will be amazed at how much good gets done.

Selectivity

In the old TV show *Maverick,* just about every week somebody would demand a showdown with Bret or Bart. But how often did they actually fight? Hardly ever. Bret and Bart were smarter than that. They knew there were better, and far safer, ways to get what they wanted.

The lesson is simple: You don't have to fight every battle. That basic truth is hard for morally angry people to learn. It's so tempting to fight for truth and justice, to climb on the chair of moral superiority. It's all too easy to slip on that robe of righteous indignation.

Alcoholics Anonymous has a simple slogan: "attraction, not promotion." The idea is that just because you have stopped drinking and found a way to stay sober that includes emotional and spiritual growth, you don't need to preach to other people to do the same. Believe your truth, but don't "promote" it by preaching, yelling, or getting up on that darn chair. All you have to do is *live* your truth. If it works, people will see you becoming happier, and they will want some of the same stuff you have. When they ask, you can tell them your beliefs. Let others fight their own battles, until they are ready to ask. That is also the time they will be ready to listen and really hear what you have to say.

Change calls for personal discipline. Here's an idea that will help.

Take three pieces of paper small enough to fit in your pocket or purse. Label them 1, 2, and 3. This is your entire moral anger quota for the week. You can only take three moral stands this entire week, so you better be choosy. And be extra careful about using the last one. If you waste it on criticizing your partner about his or her choice of breakfast cereals, what will you do if something more serious comes up?

Next week cut yourself down to two slips of paper. Then one. But don't go down to zero. Everyone needs to be able to get morally angry once in a while. Of course, just because you have that slip in your pocket doesn't mean you have to use it.

Notice we're not saying you should never get morally angry. But be selective. Think of moral anger as money. Don't squander it on useless fights. Spend it well, instead, by reserving it for really important issues.

12

Resentment/Hate

Resentment: to feel offended by something another person said or did.

Hate: an intense, unending loathing of someone.

Self-hate: an intense, unending loathing of yourself.

We've saved the topic of resentment and hate until last for a reason. Resentment combines many of the features of other kinds of anger. Resenters often hide their anger from others like anger sneaks. But they can also explode in rage. They can become addicted to the feelings of power that go with hate. And they can believe that their anger is justified, like those with moral anger.

This chapter is about resentment and hate. Think of resentment as the *beginning* and hate as the *ending* of a process in which people feel injured and offended by another person's words or deeds. They become angry. Maybe they try to take action, to get through the unhappiness. But nothing works. They get stuck. They obsess, thinking over and over about how that person hurt them. They become trapped in their anger. They just cannot let go.

Not every resentment turns into hate. Resentments are lower key. When Janine says, "I really resent the way Molly gossiped about me to the whole staff. I don't want to talk with her right now," Janine is resentful but not hateful. She has plenty of time to get through her anger. Gradually, she'll probably feel more relaxed around Molly, especially if Molly quits gossiping. But now listen to Janine a year later: "I absolutely despise Molly. She's stupid and bad and mean. She gossips all the time. Nobody trusts her. When Molly walks in the door, I walk out!" That is hatred. Hate is stronger, longer, and meaner than resentment. While resentments usually fade over time, hatreds endure and even grow more powerful.

Hate is a powerful, scary weapon. Haters can and do kill. They attack the people they hate. If they are full of self-hate, they attack and sometimes kill themselves.

One of the most striking features of hate is how long it lasts. Hate can go on forever. How often have you heard or said to yourself, "I will never forgive and never forget what he/she/they did to me"? That refusal to change is hate's trademark. Hate is a long-term problem because, once formed, it won't go away. Haters become trapped in their hate, unable to go on with their lives.

Everyone can hate. Perhaps almost everyone has hated from time to time. Hate is part of what Sigmund Freud called the love/hate relationship. The very people we most love are the ones we can most hate. Even children as young as one or two years old can hate, although a child's "I hate you" is different from a grown-up's. The child usually means, "I hate you right now, but I'll get over it soon." The adult means, "I hate you now and maybe forever. This feeling is going to last a long time."

Both love and hate are passions. They are intense, tenacious feelings. That means people who hate are very involved with their enemies. They can't let them out of their mind. The opposite of love, by the way, isn't hate. Indifference is the opposite of both love and hate. That's why the healing of hate often involves simply letting go.

"It's amazing, Pat, but I just don't think about Jimmy anymore. I used to stay up nights plotting ways to get back at him. Now I don't much care what happens to him. I have too many other things to do."

Almost everyone has felt resentment in their lives. Many have felt hate as well. And some people are constant haters. For them, hate has become their life. They are consumed by their hatreds, eaten alive as they think about past injustices, seek revenge, and act like victims. These people are stuck in hatred. They need to learn how to let go.

HOW RESENTMENT AND HATE FORM

Think of hate as a raging river. Plunging down jagged mountains, the river sweeps everything in its path. The river of hate is too strong to swim in. Try it and you'll drown. It's too dangerous to cross, too treacherous to sail on. Its only purpose seems to be to destroy.

Rivers don't usually just rise up from the ground. Many feeder springs—small creeks and streams—join to form the whole. That's true for the river of hate. Each of those streams has a name.

The first stream is named Injury. Someone says or does something thoughtless, hurtful, or mean. Or perhaps the resenter just thinks somebody is doing those things. Resentments can build up over imagined insults and misunderstandings as well as real attacks. These injuries are hard to swallow. They hurt too much to ignore.

The second stream is called Obsession. That means they can't quit thinking about the bad things people have done to them. People who obsess continually bleed from old wounds. Every time they think of what someone did to them they hurt again, sometimes even more than they did originally. They carry grudges for long periods. They refuse to forgive, because then they'd have to get on with their lives.

The third stream is called Victim Logic. Haters believe they are victims of others' evil deeds. They also think they are helpless to change their lives. It's as if someone threw them into the river and won't let them climb out.

Recently Ron saw a new client, Andrea, who was full of complaints. Andrea's husband was a jerk. Her son and daughter treated her like a doormat. Her employer made her work overtime when she was exhausted. On and on she went. Andrea was as bitter as horseradish, as acid as lemon. Everyone picked on her. So what did she want to do about all this injustice? Nothing. "Ron, I've just come to complain. I can't do anything. I'm trapped. But I'm so mad I could kill them all." Andrea preferred being a victim to taking responsibility for her own life.

Intensity is the fourth stream that feeds the river of hate. That feeling of hate is so powerful! It makes people feel alive, energetic. Just get haters talking about someone they hate to see what we mean. Suddenly their voices get louder. They gesture wildly. Their eyes gleam. Their words tumble out as fast as they can talk. Somehow it seems they get a little pleasure out of their pain, especially when they think of what they'd like to do to those they hate.

Vengeance is yet another feeder stream. Vengeful people are always plotting. Haters spend hours, days, weeks dreaming up ways to make their enemies pay. Pour sugar in their gas tanks. Steal the kids. Destroy their car. Make them look stupid.

Edgar Allan Poe is the master of revenge fantasies. Remember how his hero, in *The Cask of Amontillado*, got his rival drunk and proceeded to brick him into a wine cellar? "Now I'll make him suffer like I've suffered" is the revenge taker's goal. "Who's Sorry Now?" is their theme song.

Sometimes the river of hate is more like a glacier. It moves incredibly slowly but crushes everything in its path. There are two reasons for this. The first is that haters live in the past. The second is that they refuse to let go of their anger.

Haters live in the past. Indeed, haters don't change their view of the other person. Their minds get locked into one position and then rust shut. Once that happens their judgment of the other person can never change. "Oh, sure, he's been good since he got out of prison. But you just watch. I know what he's really like. He'll always be the same."

Haters mull over their past wounds, each time reliving them just as if they were happening right now. Sometimes the wounds are terrible: affairs, thefts, addictions, beatings, incest, deceits. But haters can get equally upset over minor scenes, such as being snubbed at a party or one thoughtless thing someone said or did. "Just look what they did to me! Look again! Again!" They'll be there long after every-one else has gone to bed, still staring at the images of their own humiliation.

Haters store up and replay three kinds of wounds. First are the things people have done to them. We call these *commissions*. These are actions, such as a spouse's affair, or insults, such as being called "selfish" or "stupid." Haters also recall the times others failed to be nice to them—or simply failed to meet their expectations. We call these *omissions*. The times someone could have said "I love you" but didn't. The Christmas card that was never sent. The forgotten "Thank you for . . ." Haters use omissions to tell themselves that they are being treated unfairly or "forgotten."

Finally, a third type of injury that is special to hating relationships is the *shortfall*. A shortfall occurs when the people you hate try to make things better, but you decide their actions are too little, too late. For example, Melvin, now twenty-five, was abandoned by his father Jim when he was about ten years old. Last year Jim found Melvin and called him up. Jim wanted to see Mel, to restart their relationship. But Melvin refused. He'd been missing his father for fifteen years. His hate was deeply rooted. "It's too late now," Melvin says. "After all this time nothing he can do will make a difference. He'll always be the man who deserted us in my mind."

There's no room for change in the mind of haters. They are stuck in the past, feeling wounded over and over as they relive their pain. The result is that they refuse to let go of their anger.

Please notice we're not saying haters *can't* let go. They can, and they must if they want to get on with their lives. The problem is they *won't* let go.

Why hang on to hate? Everyone has their own reasons, of course. Habit. Fear of change. Fear of facing the unknown. Clinging to people who are gone the only way you know how, by hating them. Enjoying the intensity of the hate experience. Waiting forever for "justice" or revenge.

Whatever the reasons, the result is the same. Haters keep hating, day after day. So much of their energy gets funneled into hate, they have time for little else.

IT'S TIME TO QUIT RESENTING AND HATING WHEN . . .

Resentment, like all human emotions, has its uses. For example, resentment announces that a person has been injured and needs comfort. It can also help people leave a bad relationship. Hate clarifies a person's values: "I hated my mother so much I vowed I'd never be like her." And, oddly enough, hate keeps people in touch with those they despise. As we noted earlier, the opposite of love is indifference, not hate. People who say "I hate you" are still deeply connected with their enemy, for better or worse.

Still, resentment can easily be overdone. It can take over your life, trapping you in your past. And hate is even worse. Hate can even become your main way of existing.

Here are a few signs that hate is in control of your life:

- You think about the person you hate every day, perhaps several times a day.

- You no longer think of the person you hate all the time. But when you do you are amazed at the power of your rage. All somebody has to do is mention your enemy's name and you start to go crazy inside.

- You often tell others how badly you have been hurt. You try to convince people to take your side, to hate your enemy as much as you do.

- You think of yourself as totally good and innocent. Meanwhile, your enemy becomes all bad and evil. You have a severe case of black-and-white thinking. Nothing the other person can say or do would make a difference.

- You can't imagine who you would be if you weren't full of hate. You see yourself as someone who hates now and always will.

- You have many thoughts and fantasies of revenge, wasting much time dreaming up ways to hurt your enemy.

- You've begun to act on those fantasies, actually doing things to get revenge on another.

- You can't get on with your life. Your hate consumes so much energy, you don't have time for other things.

- Instead of healing, your old wounds keep bleeding. You can feel yourself becoming more and more bitter. The hate seems to get worse over time.

- You feel sorry for yourself. You see yourself as a helpless victim of another's meanness. You feel unable to rescue yourself.

These are the signs that hate rules your life. However, you can get rid of hate. Here's how.

LETTING GO OF RESENTMENT AND HATE

Resentments are easier to release than hatreds. Still, they can cling like Velcro to your soul if you let them. We suggest that you take the following steps to help you release your resentments:

- If possible, speak directly with the person you resent. Perhaps the two of you can clear up the problem and be done with it.

- Think of some good things the person you resent does or has done in the past. This will remind you that the person you resent is not really a terrible person while refocusing you on some positive ways the person has behaved toward you in the past.

- Put the offense that caused the resentment in perspective. In other words, how big a deal is the offense you resent? For example, did Molly's gossiping really hurt Janine, or was it merely annoying?

- Make a conscious decision to treat the person you resent in a nicer way or more respectfully than you have been doing. This will help you break the cycle where each person feels injured by the other and then either withdraws or counterattacks.

Hate is like a raging river. Like a river, hate can be dammed up. You do that by telling yourself it's bad to hate and that you should feel guilty about hating. Unfortunately, all you'll do is create a huge lake of resentments behind that dam. An anger reservoir. Sooner or later the pressure might burst the dam, no matter how strong you tried to build it. Your anger will pour through.

Letting go of hate is more difficult than letting go of resentment. You cannot just hope it will go away. You cannot put it aside, either, because, as we have just noted, hate is like a raging river.

You need to do something better than just dam up your hate. You need to make major changes in your life. You need to transform your hate into something different, something stronger. You need to use the energy of hate in new ways.

Here is a visualization that illustrates what we mean. We suggest you read it a couple times, then close your eyes and imagine it happening to you.

You are the mighty river of hate. Fed by countless streams of resentment, you surge through mountains of rage, churning your way downstream. Nothing can stand in your path. Your purpose is to destroy, to avenge. You cannot be dammed. You cannot be controlled. You are master, warrior, supreme. You go on forever.

And then you reach the ocean.

You merge with the greatness of the ocean. You have to do this. You have no choice. You try to keep hating, to fill the sea with rage. But the ocean is too vast. All that you hate is part of this sea. All that you love. They are mixed together so thoroughly that they cannot be separated. You merge with them all. You feel connected with everything in the universe, even with those you have hated. You see that you are capable of everything evil, everything good.

You feel yourself healing.

The ocean cleanses your soul. Its waters absorb your hate, taking away your pain as a mother cradles her angry baby, offering comfort. Your hate is small now, just a drop of water in an endless sea. It means nothing.

Your hate becomes part of the ocean.

The ocean dilutes it and transforms it into pure energy. Just energy. No more hate. As you become the ocean, you feel connected with something that is both you and greater than you. You are peaceful and content.

Hate must be recognized and accepted. Yet hate is small, a tiny portion of life. You must gather your hate, even embrace it as part of your being. But keep your hate in perspective. It is part of you, not everything about you.

Hate is an energetic emotion, a passion. You can use its energy to grow. Then and only then can you say that you have hated well.

"Ron, hate was all I could feel for a year. It changed me forever. I'm not the naive young man I once was. I realize now that there is much evil in the world, but also goodness. I know now I can be just as mean and awful as the person I despised. My hate showed that to me.

Now I can get on with life. I've got so much to do that I don't want to waste any more time hating."

Forgiveness

Forgiveness is the classic antidote for resentment and hate. Forgiving others for what they do to you is a gift you give yourself. The idea is to get the monkey off your back, to get on with your life.

Resentments and hate keep you from enjoying life, from seeing the goodness in others. Resentments point toward doubt, depression, and despair. They make life into a bad play with an unhappy ending.

Forgiving involves dropping your resentments and giving up all claims on your enemies. People owe you nothing when you choose to forgive. That means you must be willing to forgive with no strings attached. Don't expect the other person to forgive you back, or return to a relationship, or be nicer, or change. If you do expect anything back for your forgiving, you are just playing games. Forgiveness is not an act of manipulation. It is a personal choice. The goal is your own personal relief.

Forgiving must be done at your own pace. It isn't a *should*. It isn't an obligation. So don't let anybody tell you that you must forgive others. Certain religions stress the need and duty of forgiving others. While respecting this position, we disagree that forgiveness is a duty. Instead, we think of forgiveness as an opportunity to deepen one's life.

Forgiving is a choice. It is an act of free will. You'll know when you're ready to forgive. You'll feel slightly sick when you start complaining again about what happened. You'll feel stuck in the past but ready to change. Your heart, soul, and mind will tell you that you need to begin forgiving.

Forgiving takes time. It is a process, not a single event.

Beverly Flanigan has written an excellent book on forgiveness called *Forgiving the Unforgivable*. Flanigan interviewed people who survived terrible blows from family or other close relationships. One was betrayed by a business partner, another was a victim of incest, a third had been abandoned at an early age. Flanigan describes six stages of forgiving. We have found these stages useful in our work with individuals and couples who are trying to overcome hate.

Naming the injury. The goal of this first stage is to describe what happened and how it affected you. It helps to be able to say clearly, for example, "I am a survivor of incest. Because of what happened, I still have trouble trusting men."

Claiming. In this stage you separate your wounds from those of others. Instead of saying, "Oh, I suffered, but Joe suffered more—so let's talk about him," you can say, "I was damaged in certain ways and Joe in others. I need to talk about my pain."

Blaming the injurer. The job here is to separate your actions from those of the injurer. For example, a woman who was sexually abused as a child may feel guilty, as if she were bad for having allowed it to happen. Responsibility is redistributed in this phase. Victimizers are held accountable for their actions.

Balancing the scales. One goal of forgiveness is to regain your lost power. In this fourth stage you do whatever is necessary to undo the injury. That might include considering the injury over and done with, initiating legal action against the wrongdoer, and regaining skills and activities once lost because of the injury. For example, the female survivor of a batterer overcomes fears of speaking in public or talking with men.

Choosing to forgive. In order to continue, you must set the injurer free. This means dropping any claims against them. Getting an apology isn't important anymore. Making them pay isn't worth the trouble. It's time to look ahead, not backwards. Choosing to forgive is a conscious choice. It means letting go of the past so you can live better in the present.

Emergence of a new self. In the final stage you quit being a helpless victim. You have gained a stronger sense of control over life. In addition, Flanigan describes what she calls the Forgiveness Principle: Harm is an ever-present possibility. Harm is part of the human experience. You realize this truth and learn to deal with adversity, even when the meaning or purpose of pain seems to make no sense. Perhaps God has a reason you cannot comprehend. Perhaps there is no reason at all. Whatever the case, the forgiver accepts the reality of a world that is neither always fair nor just. Scarred, wounded, maimed, the forgiver still finds an inner peace and serenity that had been missing.

Exercise: Do you need to begin the forgiving process? You can start by making a list of all the ways your resentments are harming you. Your wasted time and energy, lost sleep, distrust of the world, obsessive thoughts, time spent in revenge fantasies, and so on. Remember that forgiving is a gift you give yourself. Will you accept that gift, or will you trade it in for even more anger and hate?

We suggest you write a no-send letter to each of the people you need to forgive. Go through Flanigan's six stages: name, claim, blame, balance the scales, choose to forgive, let your new self begin to emerge.

Take your time doing this. Each letter can be written over a period of days or weeks. This letter is for you, not them. So don't mail it or read it to them.

You'll probably notice that parts of the letter are harder to write than others. That's where you'll have to do more work. Don't get mad at yourself about that, though. Forgiving is a difficult process. It's often hard and painful. But, if you stick with it, you'll be free from the prison of hate.

SELF-HATE AND SELF-FORGIVENESS

Hate isn't always aimed at others. It can also be directed at yourself. Self-hate is a terrible, self-inflicted wound. Self-haters deeply believe there is something very wrong with them.

Self-hate is a mixture of anger and shame. The messages are those we described in chapter 6 on shame-based anger: I'm no good, I'm not good enough, I don't belong, I'm not lovable, I should not be. Self-haters are very loyal to these messages. No amount of praise from others allows them to change. They remain convinced of their fundamental badness.

Self-haters refuse to forgive themselves. Their shame seems too deep, their badness too strong. They see themselves as bottomless cesspools full of something evil-smelling and awful. Don't even bother sending for the septic system man, they'd say. Nobody could remove all of the gunk in their souls.

Self-haters desperately need to learn how to forgive themselves. Too often, instead, they look for ways to punish themselves. They are masters at:

- Self-abuse (doing things like starving or cutting themselves)

- Self-sabotage ("I could have gotten an A, but I just never completed that last assignment, so the teacher flunked me instead.")

- Self-neglect (no physical or dental appointment for the last four years)

- Self-destruction (suicide attempts)

Recovery from self-hatred centers upon self-forgiveness. It is a slow, often frustrating process that can take a lifetime. For help, we suggest you read some books on shame for starters (ours are *Letting Go of Shame* and *The Secret Message of Shame*). The main goal is to accept yourself as a human being, which means accepting your flaws and weaknesses as well as your strengths.

Here are a few affirmations that can help you begin the process of turning self-hate into self-respect.

- I am a human being.

- I am not perfect but I am perfectly human.

- I am good enough just as I am.

- I will notice and accept my goodness as part of myself.

- I will take in messages of love and caring from others.

- I will treat myself as kindly as I treat others.

- I will take all of the parts of myself into my heart.

- I forgive myself for all I have done and all that I am.

You'll hate yourself much less often when you accept these statements. You'll not indulge in acts of self-abuse, self-neglect, self-sabotage, and self-destruction. Or, if you do, you'll be able to stop yourself more quickly so you can return to self-caring behavior.

13

Conclusion: Letting Go of Anger

Anger is an important emotion that tells you something is wrong. It pushes you into action. It's a messenger that you must not ignore. But anger can cause problems, especially when you get stuck in it.

We've described eleven completely different kinds of anger problems in this book, and there are certainly more. The eleven we chose cause the greatest number of difficulties for the most people. Each of the eleven can be changed, though, if you are willing to make a strong, conscious effort.

MASKED ANGER STYLES

The hidden, or masked, anger styles are hardest to recognize as anger. We began with anger avoidance. Anger avoiders fear and deny their anger. They simply don't want to own their anger. When they see that messenger coming, they head the other way. Anger avoiders most need to admit that everybody gets angry once in a while. They need to accept their own anger as part of themselves.

Then came sneaky anger. Anger sneaks let their anger come out sideways, through such actions as forgetting their promises and acting helpless. Anger sneaks frustrate others with their inactivity. Their anger sneaks out in the many clever ways they find not to do things. Anger sneaks most need to learn how to be direct with their anger.

Anger turned inward is another form of masked anger. People who handle anger in this manner too often turn it against themselves. They "stuff" their anger against others either because it is too frightening to show their anger or because they have been taught to get mad at themselves instead of at others. Also, they tend to be quite critical of themselves, always finding fault with how they act or think. These people need to give themselves permission to direct their anger more outwardly. They also need to find ways to love and appreciate themselves.

EXPLOSIVE ANGER STYLES

The explosive anger styles are dangerous, powerful, and alarming. People with these styles become very angry and lose control.

One kind of explosive anger is sudden anger. Sudden anger strikes like a tornado in the night. People with sudden anger must learn to recognize cues that their anger is building and slow down the process.

Shame-based anger is an explosive style that comes with a person's low self-esteem. The worse people feel about themselves, the more likely they are to be oversensitive to criticism and to think others are trying to belittle them. The antidote for shame-based anger is improved self-worth.

Deliberate anger is intentional. People use deliberate anger to get their way by scaring others. It's a crude technique that often backfires, but it's also hard to give up because it does work some of the time. People with deliberate anger need to learn new and better ways to ask for what they want.

The last explosive style is excitatory anger. People with excitatory anger seek out the intense feelings that come with rage. Their anger helps them feel alive and powerful. They may need to treat their anger as an addiction by making a commitment to decline all anger binges and by learning how to live life in moderation.

CHRONIC ANGER STYLES

Chronic anger styles endure for long periods, even years. They trap people in endless bouts of anger, gluing them to their anger like a fly to flypaper.

One kind of long-term anger is habitual hostility. People with this type of anger don't even think about why they are angry. They just are. Habitually hostile people need to break the habit by becoming more aware of their actions and substituting new behaviors and thoughts.

Paranoid anger is another form of masked anger. People who feel paranoid give away their anger. They are convinced others are furious with them, when they are really the ones who are irate. Paranoids must take back their own anger, and learn to be careful with it, before they can get better. They must also learn to trust.

Moral anger, another type of chronic anger, comes to people who defend their anger by convincing themselves they are right and good while their opponents are both wrong and bad. To escape this prison, people must let go of their feeling of superiority. They must learn to treat others as equals even when they disagree.

Finally, we described resentment, hate, and self-hate. Haters store up resentments and treat themselves as helpless victims. Self-haters despise themselves for what they see as their weaknesses. Both live in the past and cannot enjoy life. They need to learn how to forgive themselves and others.

HEALTHY ANGER

People who handle their anger well do eight things with their anger.

1. They are flexible, using more than one anger style to deal with difficult situations.

2. They treat anger as a normal part of life.

3. They use anger as a signal that there are problems they need to address.

4. They take action when necessary, but only after they've carefully thought through the situation.

5. They express their anger in moderation, without losing control.

6. Their goal is to solve problems, not just to express their feelings.

7. They state their anger clearly, in ways that others can understand, so that others can respond appropriately to their wants and needs.

8. Finally, they let go of their anger, rather than hang on to it once the problem is over.

Each anger style poses a challenge if your goal is to handle anger well. That's why it is important to understand your personal anger style or styles. The more you know about your patterns of thinking and acting, the more control you will have over your life. You can indeed learn to let go of excessive anger and resentment.

LETTING GO OF ANGER

Anger is a part of life. Our wish for you, and for ourselves, is to be able to accept the blessing of anger, to listen to its message, and then to let go of it.

Ronald T. Potter-Efron, MSW, Ph.D., and Patricia S. Potter-Efron, MS are clinical psychotherapists in Eau Claire, WI. Dr. Potter-Efron specializes in anger management while Ms. Potter-Efron focuses upon depression and substance abuse. Together they have written several books including *Letting Go of Anger, Letting Go of Shame, Reclaiming Your Relationship* and *The Treatment of Shame and Guilt in Alcoholism Counseling.* Ron has also written *Angry All The Time, Stop The Anger Now,* and *The Handbook of Anger Management* as well as *Shame, Guilt, and Alcoholism.* The Potter-Efrons teach at the Rutgers Summer School of Alcohol and Drug Studies and frequently facilitate seminars for professionals and the general public on the topics of anger management, shame and guilt, and the addictive process.

OTHER HELPFUL TOOLS FOR ANGER

Stop the Anger Now, Item 2574, $17.95

Angry All the Time, 2nd ed, Item 3929, $13.95

The Secret Message of Shame, Item 1705, $13.95

Letting Go of Anger, Item 0016, $14.95

Working Anger, Item 1195, $12.95

ACT on Life, Not on Anger, Item 4402, $17.95

Transforming Anger, Item 352X, $12.95

Freeing the Angry Mind, Item 4380, $14.95

When Anger Hurts, 2nd ed, Item 3449, $16.95

When Anger Hurts Your Kids, Item 0458, $13.95

When Anger Hurts Your Relationship, Item 2604, $13.95

Anger Control Workbook, Item 2205, $17.95

available at bookstores nationwide

To order, call toll free, **1-800-748-6873,** or visit our online bookstore at **www.newharbinger.com**. Have your Visa or Mastercard number ready.

Prices subject to change without notice.